CHILDREN OF POVERTY

STUDIES ON THE EFFECTS
OF SINGLE PARENTHOOD,
THE FEMINIZATION OF POVERTY,
AND HOMELESSNESS

edited by

STUART BRUCHEY
UNIVERSITY OF MAINE

A GARLAND SERIES

IDENTITY
AND
POVERTY

DEFINING A SENSE OF SELF
AMONG URBAN ADOLESCENTS

LAURA DeHAAN
SHELLEY MacDERMID

GARLAND PUBLISHING, INC.
NEW YORK & LONDON / 1996

Library of Congress Cataloging-in-Publication Data

DeHaan, Laura, 1964–
    Identity and poverty : defining a sense of self among urban
adolescents / Laura DeHaan & Shelley MacDermid.
        p.   cm. — (Children of poverty)
    Includes bibliographical references and index.
    ISBN 0-8153-2622-X (alk. paper)
    1. Urban poor-—United States—Psychology. 2. Poor teenag-
ers—United States—Psychology. 3. Identity (Psychology) in
adolescense—Social aspects—United States. I. MacDermid,
Shelley, 1959–   . II. Title. III. Series.
HV4045.D45 1996
305.23'5—dc20   96-36694

Printed on acid-free, 250-year-life paper
Manufactured in the United States of America

Contents

Preface

It is impossible to live in current society and not hear about the strong challenges that youth face in this country. American adolescents are facing unprecedented challenges, such as gang violence, AIDs and substance use, and are being asked to make difficult choices concerning these issues at younger and younger ages. Perhaps one of the most potentially dangerous environments for today's teens is within inner cities, where crime and poverty are serious problems.

One of the things that has always been striking to us is the fact that even though today's adolescents are faced with such difficult choices, most adolescents are able to handle the transition from childhood to adulthood very well. Even adolescents growing up with very adverse circumstances are usually able to grow into confident and competent adults. One of the goals of this project was to examine the kinds of factors help adolescents succeed, particularly those living in a risky environment, such as an inner city.

This book examines an important developmental transition: the formation of identity, as well as the influence that having a well developed identity may have, on a sample of 102 eighth graders living in urban Chicago. We found that although growing up in poverty does hamper identity development, creating a strong sense of self is an important protective factor for these adolescents who are living in an environment characterized by high stress. Creating a strong sense of identity as associated with lower levels of risk, particularly for behavioral outcomes. We also find that measuring identity development within specific domains makes an important contribution to our knowledge of how identity relates to outcomes for early adolescents.

This project was made possible by a grant from the Purdue Research Foundation at Purdue University and many people played a crucial role in the completion of this project. The first author is especially indebted to Shelley MacDermid for giving constant support to this project and challenging me to grow as a scholar. I also appreciate her willingness to allow me to pursue a whole new area of study that was somewhat unfamiliar to all of us. Thanks also go to Judith Myers-Walls, David Fasenfest, and Gail Melson who served on my dissertation commitee, for competent help and expertise. We are also grateful for Ellen Smith, Tom Ritter, and Todd and Julie Weiland for competent help in data gathering, and to Laura's husband Mike, for providing much computer support all throughout this project. Greatest thanks are of course due to the school systems, parents, and teens who allowed us to complete this project and for sharing their lives with us.

— *Laura DeHaan & Shelley MacDermid*

Identity and Poverty

I

Identity and Poverty

Over fourteen million children and adolescents in the United States, about 22% of all American children and adolescents, live in poverty (Dinitto, 1995). An even higher percentage of urban children and adolescents live with economic hardship. Wilson (1987) reports that 58% of all urban white families and 75% of all urban black families earn under 11,000 dollars a year. This compares to national rates of 13% for white families and 18% for black families.

As the number of individuals living in urban poverty increased (59% from the years 1969 to 1982), concern about people in these environments, particularly youth, also increased (Wilson, 1987). Considerable efforts have been made to ascertain the effects of economic hardship on physical and mental health (Bolger, Patterson, Thompson and Kuperschmidt, 1995; Huston, McLoyd and Coll, 1994).

Thompson (1992) argues that poverty alone "does not cause adverse developmental outcomes. However, the consequences of experiencing the conditions associated with growing up in poverty are not in doubt" (p. 7). He cites poor nutrition, lack of access to medical care, unsafe living conditions, exposure to drugs, and high crime rates as some of the problems associated with urban poverty. Garmezy (1992) also notes many risk factors associated with children living in urban poverty, risks often beginning in infancy. Low birth weight and higher rates of infant mortality are among the common problems. In a qualitative study of children in five cultures that were deemed "war zones" because of the intense violence and uncertainty of life for children, Garbarino, Kostelny, and Dubrow (1991) described inner-city Chicago as more dangerous and stressful for children than places such as Cambodia, Nicaragua, or Palestine!

> In gang-controlled communities the enemy is not so
> easily identified....Since there is little perceived societal
> support for the people trapped in these communities, the
> ability to unite around common goals and maintain
> family and cultural ties is weak...Because the enemy
> remains faceless, active coping mechanisms and
> community wide response are undermined. (pp. 146-
> 147).

Poverty has been associated with elevated levels of loneliness and depression in rural adolescents (Lempers, Clark-Lempers, and Simons, 1989), as well as school dropout rates in national studies of adolescence (Sum and Fogg, 1991). Economically disadvantaged adolescents report greater numbers of negative life events (Gad, Treadwell, and Johnson, 1980), and over 75% of all poor children and adolescents have below average basic skills in reading and math, with 50% in the lowest quintile (Sum and Fogg, 1991).

However, based on a review of research done on economic pressure and family lives, Voydanoff (1990) concludes that "relationships between economic distress and children's health and adjustment are also influenced by mediating factors. These include economic strain, parental adjustment and behavior, and gender of the child" (p. 1109). Specifically regarding adolescence, previous studies demonstrate that experiencing poverty doesn't automatically lead to poor adolescent adjustment, particularly if the family unit remains strong and provides nurturing behaviors (Huston, McLoyd and Coll, 1994; Larzelere and Patterson, 1990).

Most research on youth living in urban poverty has focused on problem behaviors: drug use (Bettes et. al., 1990), delinquency (Howard, Broquet and Farrell, 1991), and dropping out of school (Patterson, Kupersmidt, and Vaden, 1990). Although these problems are certainly worthy of research effort, the heavy priority accorded them creates a somewhat distorted picture of adolescent urban life, and ignores the more basic question of how adolescent development proceeds in these environments (Williams and Kornblum, 1985).

Even though life circumstances connected with urban poverty often are associated with high levels of stress (Dubrow and Garbarino, 1989), Garmezy (1983) maintains it is important to examine protective as well as risk factors when studying populations characterized by poverty. Links between poverty and delinquency (Larzelere and Patterson, 1990), and substance use, for example, (Fawzy, 1987) are not compelling, indicating the presence of strong mediating and protective factors. The support of family members and others, as well as individual feelings of competency, have been found as protective factors(Compas, 1987).

Completion of developmental tasks may also serve to buffer individuals against stress. Identity development, the formation of a consistent sense of self, is considered the chief developmental task of adolescence (Erikson, 1963, 1985). Identity development is defined as the ability to explore choices and then select important commitments to individuals and institutions, maintain loyalty to these commitments, and arrive at a relatively stable self-perception. Identity development relates to several important outcomes for white, middle class populations, such as adolescent autonomy (Dellas and Jernigan, 1991) and family functioning (Sabatelli and Mazor, 1985).

The development of a strong ideological identity can be an important factor relating to adjustment for adolescents living in stressful contexts such as urban Chicago, (Garbarino, Kostelny, and Dubrow, 1991):

> One source of mental health is a compelling and consistent story that bolsters the individual's sense of self-worth, that offers a basically comprehensible picture of the world, and ... the future. One aspect of narrative that enables children to survive emotionally ... is ideological, offering a world view that makes sense of experiences (p. 22).

Despite the importance of identity, its development in urban adolescents has not been studied sensitively. In fact, individual factors as a whole, regardless of their demonstrated importance in predicting resilience to stress (Sroufe and Rutter, 1984), have been largely ignored in a body of research which instead focuses on structural family variables. These variables, such as number of parents or birth order, ignore the process factors that are often found to be more predictive of adjustment (Bronfenbrenner, 1986). Voydanoff (1990) describes most research in the area of poverty and adjustment as either large scale demographic studies (for example, Rumberger, 1983) or small sample studies that are qualitative in nature (Kotlowitz, 1991; Williams and Kornblum, 1985). She argues that middle-range studies are better suited to provide assessments of economically disadvantaged individuals, in that they can take a more in-depth look at contextual factors than large studies, and are more systematic and generalizable than purely qualitative research.

Consistent with Voydanoff's recommendation, this study will examine the relationship between identity development and psychosocial adjustment for adolescents living in urban poverty. Understanding how identity development, as expressed in the multiple role domains of family, friends, academics, work, religion, and ethnicity, is related to overall adolescent adjustment, not only will increase understanding of the identity process itself, but will also assist in identifying characteristics of urban adolescents who are capable of thriving in a challenging environment. This study proposes that identity commitment, exploration, and continuity will be associated with positive psychological and behavioral outcomes for adolescents.

II

Context of Urban Poverty

THE IMPORTANCE OF CONTEXT

According to ecological perspectives (Bronfenbrenner, 1986; Lewin, 1951), experiences cannot be understood apart from the specific contexts in which they occur. Two important ideas emerge from this theoretical perspective to inform the current study. First is the importance of individual perceptions of events. Not only are experiences themselves important, but equally important are individuals' perceptions of these events. Lewin stresses "the primacy of the phenomenological over the real environment in steering behavior" and maintains that it is impossible to understand "behavior solely from the objective properties of an environment in which behavior is described without reference to its meaning for the person" (in Bronfenbrenner, 1977, p. 204). In other words, research must not only document the circumstances of an individual's life, but must also examine how individuals perceive these experiences.

A second contribution that ecological perspectives make to the study of urban poverty is in the attention given to the complexity of contexts. Bronfenbrenner (1986, 1989) maintains that psychological research should move away from simplistic categorizations of environments. He describes what are called "social address" models of research, which ignore process variables and instead impose superficial labels (such as racial group), ignoring how such categories are perceived by individuals. Social address models differentiate between groups of individuals, without attending to the unique environments or experiences of these individuals. Larzelere and Patterson (1990), in their study of delinquent boys, employed a "social address" model, as they determined economic status based on parental income alone, and did not examine individual perceptions of family economic resources.

Bronfenbrenner calls for "person-process-context" models, which examine not only the effects of context on the processes of development, but also individual factors which may also influence these processes or outcomes. An example of research conducted under this model is a study by Lempers, Clark-Lempers, and Simons (1989), of adolescents living in rural poverty. They examined individual factors such as gender and family composition, processes of perceived parental treatment, and a definition of context that included an in-depth look at economic hardship. This model was superior in that it could demonstrate both direct effects of economic hardship, as well as indirect effects, which in this case were mediated by perceived parental treatment. Their economic hardship scale was also used as a continuous variable, to avoid simplistic categorizations like "low" and "middle" classes.

Research on poor, urban adolescents has been dominated by research under the "social address" model. Lower class adolescents are usually grouped in a single category, without examining specific aspects of their environments, such as neighborhood quality or their family's ability to meet basic needs. Greater understanding of economically disadvantaged adolescents cannot occur until a more in-depth investigation of socioeconomic status occurs. Bronfenbrenner stresses the need to "penetrate behind the label of socioeconomic status," and identify specific features of social environments which are salient to a particular outcome (1986, p. 735). It thus is important for the current study to employ a more comprehensive assessment of context for adolescents living in urban poverty. It also is important to examine not only purely objective measures of poverty, such as income, but also individual perceptions of economic circumstances.

The Context of Urban Poverty

Garbarino, Kostelny and Dubrow (1991) compare life in urban cities to a war zone. They cite increasing levels of gang violence, lack of basic health care needs, inadequate food, inferior schooling, and social isolation as factors which make the context of urban poverty a stressful one. One study found that, by the time most urban children reached high school, 40% had witnessed a shooting, 33% had seen a stabbing, and 25% had personally witnessed a murder (Kotulak, 1990).

Wilson (1987), in *The Truly Disadvantaged*, describes several changes which have led to a sharp decline in the quality of urban life. First, there has been an increase in the overall numbers of youths aged 18-24 in urban cities. The median age for blacks in urban environments is 23.9, compared to 21.8 for Hispanics, and 30.3 for whites. This increase of youth has corresponded with an increase in unemployment and crime. A second factor has been a shift in the American economy from a labor economy to a service economy. This has resulted in fewer skilled labor positions, and a considerable decline in the value of a high school diploma. Often, the only career options for inner-city youth are unskilled, low paying positions or high-paying criminal activities. A third factor is the concentration of poverty in urban settings, especially for minorities. In previous years, individuals with differing levels of economic resources lived close to each other, which helped ensure that businesses, churches, and health services would have enough resources to remain in inner-city environments. The migration of middle and upper class individuals from inner-cities to the suburbs has vastly depleted the availability of these services. Currently 7% of whites live in areas where at least 40% of the neighborhood lives in poverty, as opposed to 39% of blacks and 32% of Hispanics. A final reason offered by Wilson is a lack of positive role models in neighborhoods, especially for black males. Others describe the lack of role models as a "culture of disengagement" (Taylor, 1991).

> An increasingly important factor contributing to the problem, particularly among black males, is the paucity of positive role models with whom they can identify and from whom they can acquire the knowledge, guidance, values, and skills so essential for positive identity development and sense of direction (p. 141).

Due to high rates of unemployment and large numbers of female headed families, men often play marginal roles in these environments. One response to the stressors of this environment has been what Garbarino, Kostelny, and Dubrow (1991) describe as "terminal thinking". This can be seen in the prevalence of inner-city children "playing funeral" as well as reckless and self-destructive behavior exhibited by youth. In an interview with one Chicago teenager, Kotlowitz (1991) asked the adolescent what he wanted to be when he grew up. The boy replied that he wanted to be a bus driver, *if* he grew up.

Another aspect of terminal thinking is an avoidance of thinking or planning for the future. One counselor in an inner-city school observes, "What I find mostly is students not thinking that far ahead.... They don't think about tomorrow. Unfortunately, rather than living in a dream world, many of our students suffer from lower expectations" (in Auletta, 1982, p. 242).

Clearly the context of urban poverty places children and adolescents at risk for negative outcomes. Yet, over 65% of these adolescents are able to make the transition to young adulthood and improve their living circumstances so that they are no longer living in urban poverty (Sum and Fogg, 1991). It is important to discover what resources adolescents use to make this transition successfully, and determine the role of normal developmental growth in buffering against stress.

Economic hardship, while often associated with negative outcomes for adolescents, does not automatically doom an adolescent to a low quality of life. Several factors are present which serve to buffer individuals against negative outcomes. Learning more about these factors may prove to be a critical component of future intervention programs. It is especially important to seek to identify the factors capable of protecting adolescents from the stressors of their particular context.

The Importance of Perceived Parental Treatment

As stated previously, economic hardship has been associated with several psychological and behavioral outcomes for adolescents (Gad and Johnson, 1980; Lempers, Clark-Lempers, and Simons, 1989). As stated previously, the context of urban poverty is often linked to poor adolescent adjustment. However, these effects are usually *indirect* effects, which indicates that it is not so much the environment itself, but factors which are affected by this environment, that shape developmental outcomes. One of the critical mediating factors is adolescents' perceptions of parental treatment. It is thus important to examine not only economic hardship, but how this connection is mediated by adolescent perception of parental treatment.

Research on the effects of poverty on families has taken advantage of a comprehensive study begun in 1929 in California. This yearly longitudinal study was administered between the years of 1929 to 1945, and covered the years of the Great Depression. This allowed researchers to examine family dynamics before and during the time that many families experienced heavy economic loss and pronounced economic change. In analyses of parent and child data, Elder, Liker and Cross (1984) concluded that economic hardship was associated with only two types of poor adjustment in children: temper tantrums and difficult behavior. This, however, was seen as an indirect effect, occurring through increased arbitrary and inconsistent disciplining by fathers. Irritability in mothers tended to produce defiant and aggressive behaviors in children, although this irritability was not influenced by economic loss. The fathers who increased arbitrary discipline after economic loss were more likely to have less marital satisfaction and poorer relationships with their children *before* the Great Depression, with economic changes serving to further strain family relationships for these fathers.

Another analysis of these data (which was collected from parents, children, and clinical observations) looked specifically at three factors: the role of father involvement, the role of children in shaping the relationship, and gender differences (Elder, Nguyen, and Caspi, 1985). The authors found that economic hardship increased fathers' rejecting behaviors, which damaged peer relationships for girls, but increased peer identification for boys. Physical attractiveness was related to less rejecting behavior of fathers towards their daughters, but had no effects on the father-son relationship. These studies suggest that effects of poverty are strongly mediated by familial interaction. These findings also suggest a reciprocal relationship, in that child characteristics can influence parenting behaviors.

The importance of families in mediating the effects of poverty has been shown in other studies. Lempers, Clark-Lempers, and Simons (1989) examined both the direct and indirect effects of economic hardship on rural midwestern families in the 1980s. Path analyses indicated that economic hardship had a direct effect on loneliness and depression for both male and female adolescents, but only an indirect effect on delinquency or drug use, moderated by consistency of perceived parental discipline. There was also an indirect effect of hardship on loneliness and depression, moderated by parental nurturance. Gender differences were not present. These studies clearly demonstrate the mediating role played by the family.

PROTECTIVE FACTORS

Studies using a contextual model would examine features in a given environment which either accelerate or inhibit certain outcomes. In examining patterns of individual adaptation across the life span, certain circumstances often are associated with either the onset or inhibition of later problems. These circumstances are described respectively as risk and protective factors. Kimchi and Schaffner (1990) define risk factors as those which, if present, increase the likelihood of a person developing an emotional or behavioral problem at some point in their life. The context of urban poverty has been argued to place adolescents at risk for negative outcomes (Luthar and Zigler, 1991). Protective factors are defined as attributes of individuals and environments which serve as buffers between a person and stressful situations. As stated previously, positive family interaction has been shown to be protective for adolescents.

Based on reviews of research, Garmezy (1984) has developed three broad classes of protective factors: 1) the child possessing an easy-going or positive disposition, 2) a family environment in which at least one of the caregivers provides support, and 3) the child being able to make use of an external system of support (such as teachers, counselors, ministers, etc.). Rutter (1987) argues that it is impossible to identify unchanging risk and protective factors, and that these factors must be examined within the context of a person's life. Events such as parental death or divorce do not influence everyone equally. Timing of experience, the person's temperament, social support and other factors influence how stressful events are experienced. Likewise, having a close and supportive relationship with parents may serve as a protective factor for most situations, but may make the transition of death or divorce more difficult. In a longitudinal study of 740 urban junior high school students, Connell, Clifford, and Crichlow (1991) found that economic hardship was associated with negative school outcomes more strongly for girls, while neighborhood quality was more strongly associated with negative outcomes for boys. This focus on the contextual nature of protective factors is consistent with arguments offered by Bronfenbrenner (1986).

Several studies have examined economically disadvantaged children and adolescents from the standpoint that their environment places them at risk; in fact Luthar (1991) maintains that SES is the most commonly examined childhood and adolescent risk factor. Some identified risks related to economic hardship are low status parental occupation, large family size, minority group membership, and being raised in a one-parent home. However, in a review of this literature, Luthar and Zigler (1991) argue that methodology assessing socioeconomic status is often simplistic. Beale-Spencer and Markstrom-Adams call for developmental models of risk and protective factors which are sensitive to the specific environments of racial minorities and economically disadvantaged adolescents, instead of assuming homogeneity for these diverse groups.

Most studies on low SES populations have dwelt on risk, rather than protective factors, and on problems rather than successes. This problem-focused research has concentrated on the detrimental effects of poverty to human development. However, it is possible the relationship between poverty and development are reciprocal instead of unidirectional. The completion of developmental tasks may well create important resources and strategies that are effective buffers against stressful contexts.

Instead of problem-oriented studies, it may be advantageous to follow in the footsteps of mainstream adolescent research and examine normative developmental issues and transitions. Little is known about identity development, transitions to puberty, formal operational development, or adolescent ego-centrism in disadvantaged youth. Examining how poor adolescents negotiate these developmental tasks would provide insight not only into these populations, but would also add to overall understanding of development. Understanding commonalties and differences among racial and class groups represents an exciting opportunity for those interested in adolescents, because true developmental themes can emerge. If, for example, individuals undergo similar identity development processes, regardless of ethnicity or economic resources, researchers can be more confident that these phenomena are more truly developmental, rather than culturally bound occurrences.

This study will examine several risk and protective factors. Risk factors will include high levels of poor perceived parental treatment and higher levels of economic hardship. Positive perceived parental treatment and higher levels of identity development will also be hypothesized to be protective.

EXAMINING DEVELOPMENTAL ISSUES AMONG URBAN ADOLESCENTS

When examining developmental issues among adolescents living in urban poverty, it is important to select a theoretical framework which can examine adolescents' lives both sensitively and comprehensively. Three criteria have been selected to evaluate the effectiveness of theories for the current study. The theory needs to be sensitive to differences in context, and should attend to the unique stressors and circumstances in the lives of the urban poor. Secondly, the theory needs to examine not only the aspects of urban life which threaten successful adolescent development, but also those factors which enhance adolescent development (both risk and protective factors). Finally, the theory needs to be broad enough to examine several domains of an adolescent's life, in that adolescence is a time in which profound change occurs in many arenas, such as family, school and peer relationships. Possible theories include those of Piaget, Kohlberg, Loevinger, and Blos.

Piaget's (1930) four-stage theory of cognitive development is not particularly well suited to examine developmental issues for urban adolescents, as it does not meet any of the three criteria at a high level. This theory focuses on biological maturation and stresses the universality of cognitive stages, thus minimizing contextual differences. Although cultural differences are acknowledged in terms of when cognitive reasoning is reached, the process of cognitive development itself is argued to be universal. In other words, there may be quantitative, but not qualitative cultural differences. This theory does not provide enough focus on examining risk and protective factors for a given population. Another limitation is the somewhat narrow focus. Even though the importance of peers is acknowledged in cognitive development, this theory concentrates only on mental reasoning. While cognitive development is certainly an important task for adolescents, this theory does not provide a suitable framework for examining the integration of psychological and social factors, or examining the multiple roles that adolescents experience.

Kohlberg's (1973) six-stage theory of moral development is subject to many of the same criticisms as Piaget's. It focuses on the development of universal levels, not contextual differences. It also does not address how moral development could serve either as a risk or protective factor for adolescents, or which factors lead to inhibition or enhancement of moral reasoning skills. As its focus on only one level of cognitive functioning is even narrower than Piaget's, it cannot examine the multiple arenas of adolescent life. It also has been suggested that biases plague this theory. Schweder (1982) maintains that Kohlberg has deemed certain values, namely liberalism, intellectualism, and secularism, as universal goals for humanity. As studies have shown that those with liberal beliefs score higher on Kohlberg's measure (Fishkin, Keniston, and MacKinnon, 1973), as do young adults attending college (Rest, 1975), claims of universality seem doubtful. It seems that scoring at the advanced or principled level of Kohlberg's scale does not deem a person moral, as much as it deems her liberal, secular, and well-educated. These biases may be especially problematic for this population, which may not receive quality education or an adequate chance to develop cognitive skills.

Loevinger's (1966) theory of ego development refers to frameworks of meaning which people use to describe their experiences. Individuals move in six stages, from a presocial stage, where they are incapable of distinguishing from self and "nonself," to more conscious conceptions of self. This theory also focuses on universal stages and does not identify which factors are associated with successful stage completion. It also does not examine multiple roles in an individual's life. As peer relationships undergo profound change during adolescence (Berndt and Savin-Williams, 1990) it is important to examine adolescent development in a framework in which the unique role of peers is acknowledged.

Blos' theory of adolescent development represents a modern interpretation of Freud's psychoanalytic theory. His theory was developed in part from clinical work with juvenile delinquents, and has less to do with normative behavior than with the examining of the etiology of deviant behavior. Blos (1979) defines adolescence as an important intersection between physical and environmental factors. He describes six stages of adolescence, beginning with Freud's latency stage and ending with the transition into adulthood.

Blos' theory does not satisfy the previously mentioned criteria needed to examine this population. It does not even acknowledge contextual differences nor how these different adolescent stages or various factors serve either to strengthen or to threaten the successful completion of these stages. It also does not provide a framework in which to examine multiple domains of adolescent life.

III

Identity Development

Perhaps one of the most important contributions to the study of adolescence has been Erikson's theory of ego-identity development. As part of his eight stage model of human development, Erikson (1963) considers identity formation to be the primary task of adolescence. Erikson maintains that ego-identity is "the accrued confidence that the inner sameness and continuity of the past are matched by the sameness and continuity of one's meaning for others" (p. 61). This sense of identity is formed through interaction with others. Individuals must compare perceptions of themselves to how others see them, and consolidate these two perceptions into one coherent image. Josselson (1987), offers this definition, "Identity, then is a dynamic fitting together of parts of the personality with the realities of the social world so that a person has a sense both of internal coherence and meaningful relatedness to the real world" (p. 12-13).

Research supports the idea that identity development begins in childhood, and undergoes considerable advancement in adolescence. Hart, Maloney, and Damon (1987), in a series of comprehensive interviews of first- through tenth-graders, found that children did possess a degree of constancy about their personal identities, but that the constancy was limited to "immutable" or physical self characteristics. It is argued that the rapid physiological and cognitive changes occurring in adolescence make it impossible for adolescents to hold onto such physical descriptions, forcing them to develop more abstract and philosophical feelings of constancy and uniqueness. Perceptions of continuity and uniqueness was found to advance considerably with age. Because of this change in self-definition, it would be expected that identity development would be tied more to actual behaviors in the junior high years, and shift to a stronger link to more internalized outcomes during the high school years.

Another study found differences in identity development between the junior high and high school years. Hart (1988) examined self-perceptions of identity in a racially mixed sample of 5th, 7th, 9th, and 11th graders, and found that junior high school students were more likely to consider their social relationships (friends and activities) as what "most clearly retained the sense of identity" (p. 105), while senior high school students considered their personality characteristics more essential in self-description.

The alternative to a formed ego-identity is termed "role confusion," which occurs when adolescents are not able to commit to definite life choices. Erikson (1985) stresses that at least some role confusion is a "normative and necessary" experience for adolescents, but it can, if an individual remains unable to move out of this period of indecision, lead to a more dysfunctional state. These adolescents will be unable to experience intimacy fully, which is Erikson's next life stage.

Several assumptions about the nature of identity are noted by Erikson. First, although identity is particularly salient during adolescence, changes can and do occur earlier in childhood and later in adulthood. Second, successful completion of a consolidated ego-identity depends in part on how earlier tasks during the life-span have been resolved. Consequently, successful consolidation of an ego-identity plays a decisive role on whether future tasks, such as intimacy or generativity, are successfully obtained. Third, optimal identity formation can occur only when adolescents take an active role in their identity search and experience a normative, psycho-social period of moratorium, when they actively try out several different roles or possibilities without making definite commitments. Fourth, identity development cannot be considered solely an individualistic process. Commitments and exploration are based in part on historical and contextual factors. Fifth, identity is neither a static nor unidimensional entity. Erikson cites five facets of identity: sexual, religious, political, ideological, and occupational identities, and believes that individuals redefine these identities throughout the course of their lives (1963).

Identity Development : Marcia's Application and Extension of Erikson's Theory

Much of the work on adolescent identity development has been conducted under the typology offered by Marcia (1966, 1980).

However, this typology does not appear to be an appropriate framework for the current study. This section will review Marcia's application and extension of Erikson's theory, as well as critiques of the typology.

In perhaps the most popular attempt to operationalize Erikson's ideas, Marcia (1966, 1980) cites two facets of identity formation, crisis (or a decision-making period), and commitment (personal investment), and has developed a typology based on these dimensions. Individuals in diffusion are those who have made no identity commitments, and are not involved in any period of crisis or exploration. Individuals in foreclosure are those who have made commitments without first undergoing a period of crisis or exploration. These commitments, although firmly held, remain child-like in nature in that no exploration of options has been considered. Moratorium represents a status in which an individual has not made commitments in terms of identity formation, but is currently exploring different options. This status is a necessary precursor to the identity-achieved status, and represents individuals who are not committed to any definite directions. Identity achievement refers to the state of reaching a well-defined commitment after a period of active exploration (Marcia, 1987).

Marcia believes, along with Erikson, that identity is one of several developmental tasks for individuals, and that successful completion of earlier tasks will in part dictate successful identity achievement. He also maintains that identity achievement is a slow process, and that the necessary "cognitive, physiological and socio-expectational" ingredients required to achieve a mature identity are not available to an individual until late adolescence (Marcia, 1987, p.5).

A considerable amount of research has attempted to operationalize the ideas of Erikson and Marcia. Marcia's four statuses have been the subject of most research in the identity status paradigm and several correlates have been found. Of the four statuses, identity achievers were found to possess higher grade point averages (Cross and Allen, 1970), and foreclosed adolescents scored significantly higher in levels of authoritarianism and conformity (Schenkel and Marcia, 1972). Students in what is described as "firm foreclosure" (i.e. remaining in foreclosure for two years or more) were more likely to seek nurturance from others (Kroger, 1995). Moratorium subjects showed the highest levels of anxiety (Podd, Marcia, and Rubin, 1970), and adolescents in either moratorium or identity achieved status were more likely to score high on measures of adolescent egocentrism (O'Connor, 1995).

Self-esteem measures, when given with the identity interview, revealed conflicting results. In an early study by Marcia (1966), identity status was very weakly correlated with self- esteem ($r = .26$). But a later study showed that females in foreclosure held the highest self-esteem, and identity-achieved subjects scored the lowest. For males, however, those in moratorium or identity achievement had the highest self-esteem scores (Marcia and Friedman, 1970).

There also appears to be a relationship between identity development and moral development. In a study which looked at identity development and Kohlberg's scale of moral reasoning, individuals in foreclosure were more conforming to societal rules, and had more respect for authority and conventional values. Moratorium individuals reported the lowest levels of authoritarianism (Marcia, 1966). Rowe and Marcia (1980), who interviewed 20 males and six females on levels of identity status and moral reasoning, found that there was a positive correlation between identity achievement and higher levels of moral reasoning, based on Kohlberg's scales. They also hypothesized that other social factors must be considered.

Past research in identity status is helpful to the current study in several ways. This body of research attests to the importance of identity and the predictive power of identity development on a variety of behavioral and psychological outcomes. However, this research has not focused on examining identity in relation to social context, nor has it acknowledged the multiple domains in which identity commitments are formed and maintained.

Critiques of Marcia's Identity Status Theory

Despite the widespread popularity of Marcia's typology of identity statuses, which has resulted in over 100 studies (Cote and Levine, 1988), many argue that this typology does not fully operationalize Erikson's ideas. Waterman maintains that the dimensions of identity have not been fully explored. "This has resulted from a tendency in both Erikson's writing, and in the research on identity (Marcia, 1980), to treat identity as a global descriptive quality. An adolescent is said either to have a clear personal sense of identity or to lack one, with each state viewed as having distinct psychological concomitants" (Waterman, 1985, p. 6). He maintains that some adolescents can develop mature political identities, for example, while not considering vocational or recreational commitments at all.

In order to explore all ranges of identity development fully, according to Waterman (1982), it is necessary to view identity as both a content and process variable. As a process variable, identity must be studied as the means or techniques an individual uses to evaluate and discern exactly what goals, values, or accomplishments are likely candidates for possible identity commitments. As a content variable, it must be recognized that identity cannot be studied independently of context, and attempts should be made to uncover the individual areas in an adolescent's life in which identity commitments are made, and develop a deeper understanding of the breadth and depth of those commitments. Grotevant (1986) suggests that the development of identity should examine specific content areas and focus on process, in that different facets of an adolescent's life will "come into focus" at different periods. For example, religious salience may peak when the adolescent is going through confirmation classes at church, and vocational concerns may heighten during senior year of high school. Grotevant also highlights the need for process-focused research because adolescents do not often remain in a particular identity status for long periods.

> The statuses . . . present difficulties when one wishes to make predictions of status from developmental variables... what variance is being accounted for when we attempt to ... predict identity status from hypothesized family antecedents? Today's moratorium or diffused subject might be identity achieved next month, yet his or her parents may not have changed (p. 178).

Grotevant (1987) also stresses the idea of identity development as being a normal process in adolescence, and calls for more concentrated study on the process of exploration, as opposed to Marcia's term "crisis". Grotevant defines identity exploration as "problem-solving behavior aimed at eliciting information about oneself or one's environment, in order to make a decision about an important life choice" (p. 204). He suggests that, even though identity development may be a time of anxiety and stress, identity development, particularly exploration, is a crucial part of human development. Although he does not discount the possibility that these explorations might involve a certain degree of stress or anxiety, he does argue that the exploration process itself is not inherently stressful, and is important to development. This model recognizes that identity development may be more concentrated in one area of life than another, and takes into account personal abilities, environmental context, and exploration.

Cote and Levine (1988) also note several limitations in Marcia's theory of identity status, and argue that it is not a true representation of Erikson's theory, despite its stated intention of operationalizing Erikson's ideas. They believe that Marcia changed the meanings of the terms used by Erikson. For example, as Erikson argues that identity is never "established" and that identity issues may continue to reach the level of crisis well into adulthood (1988), he would never refer to identity as something that had been *achieved*. As this landmark is not permanent, and represents only a period of relative calm and commitment, it is not a useful, much less developmental, stage. Erikson and Marcia also give very different meanings to the word foreclosure, as Marcia sees it as the unquestioning adoption of parental values, while Erikson used it to describe individuals whose identity search had been prematurely "aborted," such as an individual who wanted to explore a college career, but does not have necessary funds to attend college.

Cote and Levine (1987) also argue that Marcia's theory is purely psychological, while Erikson continually stresses the importance of social and historical context. Erikson's period of *moratorium* is one sanctioned by society, such as in the United States, where moratorium is a period roughly covering the second decade of life. During this societally sanctioned period experimentation is allowed and encouraged. Thus, *all* adolescents are perceived to be in moratorium. However, Marcia maintains that only those individuals who are in an active exploration period are in moratorium. This acontextual view is deemed problematic by Cote and Levine (1988), "We suggest that a point of view which takes into account the role of the *context* in which commitments are developed, and therefore does not run the risk of prematurely assuming their permanence, would allow one to see the above 'regression anomaly' as a spurious problem stemming from an acontextual notion of commitment formation" (p 171).

Their other criticisms include the fact that Marcia's theory is elitist, in that individuals are asked, "Are higher forms of psychological development available to all or are they generally restricted to the privileged and fortuitous for others?" (p. 179). Another "elitist" indication is that only college (usually white) populations have been studied, and an average of only 20% are considered achieved. The typology also leaves out many components that are important to Erikson's theory, such as continuity over time, integration, and social evaluations.

Another problem with using the identity status approach, especially for this study, is its focus on the later years of adolescence. If the college years are the most active for identity status change (Marcia, 1980; Waterman, 1985), these statuses are not as sensitive to the identity explorations of younger adolescents. As Erikson has described identity development as the chief developmental task for the whole of adolescence (not just late adolescence) it is important to focus on identity in the earlier years, not just its concluding stages.

The utility of using a model developed for white college students with a somewhat narrow focus of study may be limited for adolescents in urban poverty. A more contextually-based approach is needed in order to understand identity development for adolescents living in urban poverty. The global portrayal of the identity status does not adequately address whether or not identity is actually protective in coping with life circumstances, or whether some commitments may actually be maladaptive. Neither does it allow an examination of the many domains in which adolescent development occurs.

Identity Development as a Protective Factor

As previously stated, one of the strengths of adolescents, according to Erikson, is their capacity for fidelity to individuals or institutions. Adolescents, as a result of their search for new ideological possibilities, are eager to make strong identity commitments, at least temporarily, to new belief systems. Even though the rationale or logic behind these belief systems cannot always be articulated, it does not decrease the ardor or passion that adolescents are capable of placing to individuals or ideas.

> The evidence in young lives of the search for something and somebody to be true is seen in a variety of pursuits more or less sanctioned by society... This search is easily misunderstood, and often is only dimly perceived by the individual himself, ... must often test extremes before settling on a considered course (Erikson, 1961, pp. 3-4).

As Erikson argues that fidelity is the strength of adolescence, it could also be argued that the development of a personal sense of continuity and commitment to individuals and institutions would serve as a protective factor for adolescents. In a study of adolescents from India, Islamia (1990) found that minorities and poor adolescents had higher religious, cultural, and linguistic identities than those in the majority group, possibly indicating an increased need for a clear identity for members of minority or disadvantaged groups. What remains unclear is whether the acquisition of this clear identity is related to increased psycho-social functioning.

Garbarino, Kostelny, and Dubrow (1991) argue that the formation of a strong ideological identity is an effective buffer against extreme stress, especially if that ideology is based on tolerance for others, even an identified enemy. They write, "Humans are meaning-seeking organisms... Without meaning we tend to get lost and succumb to self-destructive or to anti-social behavior or to madness" (p. 22). This suggests that self-constructed ideologies serve to buffer against negative outcomes, both psychological and behavioral.

Even though the previous critique of identity statuses raises questions about its appropriateness for use in this study, most research which has examined whether or not identity is a protective factor has operationalized identity under the global status approach. Therefore this body of research will be briefly discussed.

In a study of 18 white adolescents (half of whom were enrolled in a special school program because of behavior problems), Protinsky and Walker (1988) found that "non-problem" adolescents scored higher in identity measures than did problem adolescents. A similar study by Arehart and Smith (1990) found that adolescents living in juvenile detention centers performed significantly more poorly on global measures of identity. Scores on the Dysfunctional Attitude Scale counted for 52% of overall variance for identity resolution. These studies demonstrated an association between identity development and increased psychosocial functioning, although causal direction is not clear. A study of boarding school male adolescents found a strong relationship between identity achievement and an absence of behavior problems (Wires, Barocas, & Hollenbeck, 1994). College students in identity achievement were found to make more planful decisions than diffused students, who made decisions more intuitively and based on the opinions of others (Blustein and Phillips, 1990).

Identity development is also associated with more functional family interaction styles. Identity resolution was found to be related to intimacy with both mothers and fathers for college students (Weinmann and Newcombe, 1990). In a study of white seventh-graders, it was found that adolescents whose mothers approved of their activities engaged in more identity exploration (Papini, Sebby, and Clark, 1989). However, the same study also indicated that a high level of emotional intimacy was negatively associated with identity search. A study by Kim, Goldstein, and Jurich (1991) found similar results in that identity-foreclosed college students were the most likely to describe their families as cohesive. As foreclosure is associated with limited exploration, it appears that emotional closeness may not be associated with high levels of identity search, even for college students. However, a study which examined college females found that individuals who reported close family relationships as well as the freedom for identity exploration scored highest in both identity exploration and commitment (Fullinwider, 1991). Another study found that identity exploration and development is more closely related to parental attachment for women than for men (Schultheiss, Palladino, and Bluestein, 1994).

Several studies have examined the relationship between adolescent substance use and identity development, as that development has been operationalized by Marcia (1966, 1980). In a study that compared junior and senior high school students from a school population to adolescents who were living in a residential treatment center for substance use, differences were found according to identity status. Jones, et. al. (1989) matched 27 junior and senior high school adolescents in the treatment center with those who were attending school in the surrounding community. Participants were matched for age, grade, ethnicity, and religious preference. Adolescents in the treatment center scored significantly lower on both identity achievement and moratorium measures, and significantly higher on foreclosure measures, which the author argues is indicative of "lower psychosocial maturity" (p. 625). However, the sample size was small, and since no drug use measures were given, it is impossible to know if the adolescents living in the treatment center were significantly different from other adolescents in terms of drug use. It is also possible that the lower identity achievement and moratorium scores are more reflective of living in an institutional environment, in that active identity exploration opportunities may be limited.

Another study conducted by Christopherson, Jones, and Sales (1988) focused not on whether individuals in different statuses used more or fewer drugs, but whether the *motivations* for using drugs were different across the identity statuses. Achieved and moratorium adolescents were more likely to cite curiosity or recreation for motivations for drug use, while diffused and foreclosed subjects cited boredom and peer drug use. Identity achieved and foreclosed subjects cited religion as a reason for non-use. Achieved and moratorium adolescents also cited lack of interest in drugs. However, these reasons were not capable of accounting for a great deal of variance (less than 10%), and frequency or severity of drug use was not tested.

A study of white and Hispanic junior high school students (Streitmatter, 1989) found that high diffusion and foreclosure scores were associated with lower math and language scores, even though diffused subjects reported fewer days missing. Adolescents in moratorium had the highest math scores, although they were the most frequently absent. This suggests that identity development, as defined by Marcia's four statuses, is related to academic achievement.

Although these studies reveal interesting associations between identity development and increased psychological, behavioral, and family functioning, generalizability across cultural context should not be assumed. Because the majority of these studies were conducted on white university students, it is difficult to determine whether these findings would be replicated in the current study. Identity development may play a different role for disadvantaged or minority adolescents.

Despite difficulties in previous research, there are indications that the development of a mature identity may indeed serve as a protective factor for adolescents. Firm and stable commitments may increase feelings of self-efficacy and aid in the development of future goals. However, it is also possible that adolescents may make commitments to people or groups that do not lead to positive outcomes, such as identification into a gang. It is important to examine factors which lead into different identity commitments, and whether identity processes actually differ across cultural contexts and content-specific domains.

CONCEPTUALIZATION OF IDENTITY FOR CURRENT STUDY

The previous review of identity literature demonstrates that many facets of this construct have been conceptualized and measured. Several alternative conceptions of identity have also been proposed by various researchers (see Appendix A for a brief discussion of several of these approaches). The current study will examine three components of this important developmental task for adolescents: fidelity, exploration, and continuity. It looks at these three components in each of six content areas: family, peers, academics, work, ethnicity, and religion.

This study accepts the definition of identity offered by Newman and Newman (1988), "This identity is a creative integration of past identifications, future aspirations, and contemporary talents and abilities that is formed within a context of cultural expectations and demands" (p. 552). It is believed that this definition focuses on both individual commitments as well as the social contexts in which these commitments are made. It also sees merit in conceptualizing identity as "set of resources and strategies which can be maneuvered or manipulated at will" (Becker, 1990, p. 49).

It is believed that these three components of identity, examined in six roles, most successfully meet the criteria of an appropriate theoretical framework to examine adolescent developmental issues in the context of urban poverty. The first reason is the theory's explicit assumption that context plays an important role in not only which identity commitments are made, but in how they are expressed. Thus, various particular environments can be examined without making fundamental changes to the theory itself. The theory also highlights both the advantages and risks of adolescent exploration and commitment. Finally, another important advantage of Erikson's theory is its focus on several domains of adolescent life. This acknowledgment of multiple areas of adolescent life, such as family, work, or faith commitments, is important while examining complexities of adolescent urban life.

Definition of Identity for Current Study

This study will examine identity development in a way believed to be consistent with Erikson's original ideas. Identity will be operationalized not as global statuses, but as a series of continua, in which adolescents express more or less identity development. Levels of identity will vary across several roles. Three key concepts of Erikson's definition of identity will be used in the definition of identity for the current study: fidelity, exploration, and continuity. These concepts will be briefly discussed.

Fidelity. An important component of identity search can be, according to Erikson, the deep commitments that are made along the way to individuals or ideas. Such commitment is termed fidelity by Erikson (1988), and is deemed the central strength of adolescence. Erikson argues that identity development cannot be attained without periods of intense (although sometimes temporary) loyalty to individuals and ideas. He writes:

> Fidelity, when fully matured, is the strength of disciplined devotion... Adolescent development comprises a new set of identification processes, both with significant persons and with ideological forces, which give importance to individual life by relating it to a living community and to ongoing history (p. 20).

Fidelity can thus be defined as loyalty and commitment to persons or institutions. This sense of commitment has been found to be an important part of ethnic (Phinney and Tarver, 1988) and religious (Gillespie, 1990; Markstrom-Adams and Hofstra, 1993) identity development, as well as global identity (Marcia, 1980; Waterman, 1985). Fidelity is similar to the term commitment in many ways, but also includes an focus on expressed pride and loyalty in being affiliated with persons or institutions, as well as a high value placed on promise-keeping and faithfulness (Kitchener, 1983).

Exploration. Another component of identity that is examined in many current measures of identity (Bennion and Adams, 1986; Marcia, 1966; and Berzonsky, 1989) is exploration. Grotevant (1987) stresses the importance of examining exploration, arguing that exploration is the process in which adolescents make important life decisions. "For adolescents, the 'work' of identity is seen in the exploration process" (1991, p. 75).

Exploration is the degree to which an adolescent has critically examined a certain identity choice. Waterman (1992) defines identity exploration as "a period of struggle or active questioning in arriving at various aspects of personal identity, such as vocational choice, religious beliefs" (p. 56). This process may involve considering other alternatives, visualizing the future both with and without this commitment, or discussing the commitments with individuals who both agree and disagree with a particular identity choice.

Although many theorists (Erikson, 1963; Marcia, 1960) have applied the term "crisis" to this period of exploration, current work tends to view this process as less anxiety-provoking. Grotevant (1987) stresses the idea that exploration is a normal process of adolescence. Although he does not discount the possibility that these explorations might involve a certain degree of stress or anxiety, he does argue that these explorations are not inherently stressful, and that the process is critical to development.

Continuity. The last component of identity to be examined in this study is continuity. Continuity is defined as a sense of stability or permanence, as well as connecting past experiences to both current self-definition and goals for the future. This sense of stability is central to Erikson's (1963, 1985) notion of identity. He argues that identity is the process by which past, present, and future experiences are knit into one coherent and continuous story.

This continuity consists of considerably more than possessing a certain belief for a long period of time. It represents a developmental push to establish "a deep sense of unity" in who we are as individuals (Blasi, 1988, p. 228). Grotevant (1992) writes, "At some level, we all know what identity means because it touches on that core sense of self that we associate with a feeling of coherence of personality and continuity over time" (p. 73). Continuity is then a system of organization which individuals employ to understand and rely on who they are.

Context-Specific Domains of Identity

Because many past studies have indicated that identity development can occur at different rates across domains (Gillespie, 1990; Grotevant, 1987; Waterman, 1985), this section discusses identity development in six domains considered important to this population, based on previous research. The domains are family commitments, peer relationships, academics, career, ethnic identity and religiosity.

Family identity

Family life remains the most powerful context during the adolescent years, even though family life changes considerably. Although this change is sometimes marked by emotional distance or conflict, adolescent connections to their parents tend to remain strong, and the quality of these relationships is predictive of a variety of behavioral and psychological outcomes.

Adolescence is being increasingly considered to have an impact on not only individuals, but the entire family as well. Levels of family conflict (Silverberg and Steinberg, 1987) and family interaction patterns (Steinberg, 1981) are found to be influenced by having one family member in adolescence. A major change in family interactions occurs in the arena of decision making, as adolescents begin to play a larger role in family decisions (Smetana, 1991). Adolescent perceptions of family power changes as well, and they tend to view the same sex parent as more powerful in family interactions (McDonald, 1982). Perhaps this is why mother-daughter conflict increases during adolescence, while father-daughter relationships remain unchanged (Steinberg, 1987).

In an overview of research done on poverty among black families, McLoyd (1990) concludes that the disruption in parents' lives leaves them less capable of functioning as parents and coping with negative life events. He argues that family dynamics are the most predictive coping factors, and that "children's adjustment to stressful life circumstances is less a matter of their personal characteristics and individual resilience than of the family in which they function" (p. 336). He calls for increased research with black populations living in poverty (as only one in seven black children lives above the poverty line), and more studies of family processes.

Although many studies have investigated parent-adolescent interaction and the influence of this interaction on well-being, less is known about how adolescents incorporate their families into their description of self. It is important to examine not only perceived parental treatment, but to also consider how adolescents identify with their families. Is family commitment and loyalty a salient issue? Do adolescents actively explore how their family is integrated into their self-definition, and is this integration developed into a stable and coherent image? Family identity, as well as perceived parental support, is an important component when trying to predict psychological and behavioral outcomes.

Peer Identity

Peer relationships are an integral part of adolescent development, and adolescent friendships are noted for their intensity and loyalty (Erikson, 1963; Berndt, 1982). In fact, same-sex friendships are considered closer and more intense during early adolescence than any other point on the life-span (Douvan and Adelson, 1966). The development of peer friendships is argued by many to play an important part in the development of adolescent autonomy. Berndt and Savin-Williams (1990) argue "friends are critical interpersonal bridges that move them [adolescents] toward psycho-social growth and social maturity" (p. 3). American adolescents currently spend nearly 20 hours a week with peers (outside of the classroom), and most adolescents describe time spent with peers as the most enjoyable (Csikszentmihalyi and Larson, 1984).

Peers may fulfill an especially role for urban environments. Taylor (1991) argues that adolescents "often find the street culture of their peers a welcome relief from the anxiety and stress associated with their other environments. For many inner-city adolescents, both male and female, involvement in peer group culture comes fairly early in life and takes on many of the socialization functions of the family" (p. 150). Taylor argues that, although peer involvement reduces anxiety and teaches adolescents how to survive in the street culture, these relationships can also place urban adolescents at risk for deviant and self-destructive activities.

In a study of 1,309 low SES, minority, urban junior high school students, Howard, Broquet and Farrell (1991) found that adolescents who spent increased time away from home were more likely to engage in delinquent acts, substance use, and premarital sex. This was true for both males and females. Bowker and Klein (1983) maintain that peers play a more influential role than families in female gang membership in low SES populations. In a interview conducted with female gang and non gang members in an urban environment, no family structural or relationship differences were present in the two groups. However, there were differences in peer involvement. Gang members were more likely to be popular with boys, engage in delinquent activities, and spend time with girl friends than non gang members.

Peer identity encompasses the degree to which adolescents feel loyal and committed to their friends, have explored what kind of friends they want to have as well as what kind of friend they want to be, and how their friends fit into their overall-self definition. Given the importance of adolescent friendship, it is likely that identity development in the role of peer relationships is important in understanding adolescent adjustment and well-being.

Academic Identity

Even though only 14% of American adolescents leave high school before receiving a diploma, in many urban high schools, fewer than one half of the students actually graduate from high school (Sum and Fogg, 1991). Dropout rates appear to be decreasing slightly among low SES and minority youth; however Blacks (19%) and Hispanics (38%) drop out of high school more often than whites (13%) (U.S. Department of Education, 1991).

Studies indicate that the context of urban poverty is associated with decreased school performance and completion rates. However, because these studies have been large-scale in nature, less is known about factors which distinguish between adolescents who do well in school and those who do not.

Little is known about how adolescents in urban poverty have integrated the role of a student into their overall perceptions of self. The salience of the student role to adolescents living in urban poverty is also unknown. It is important to distinguish between academic identity and academic achievement. Identity refers to an internal process in which an adolescent comes to see herself as a certain type of student, and the saliency of the student role to her life. The study of academic identity would show whether this perception of oneself as a student is related to actual student performance. It would also guide understanding of how adolescents in this context perceive, and feel connected with, their school.

Career Identity

Another important area in which identity is explored is deciding on a vocation. Much of Erikson's (1968) discussion of identity focused on career choice, which he considered the most critical identity choice. Career choices are an important part of self-definition, in part because work "remains a necessary condition for drawing the individual into the mainstream of social life" (Wilinsky, 1964, p. 134). Career identity formation is currently considered by many theorists to involve a life-long period of exploration that reaches particular salience during the time that high-school adolescents make the transition to young adulthood (Blustein and Palladino, 1991).

Current theories of career exploration acknowledge the influence of context on career exploration. "It must be emphasized that the potential to explore is directly related to the availability of choices. When economic necessities force an adolescent to earn a living, exploration is a luxury that cannot be afforded. In addition, societal or familial values about decision making may constrain or facilitate the exploration process" (Grotevant and Cooper, 1987, p. 236). Sum and Fogg (1991) argue that even though many poor urban youth are able to become successfully employed, "... the journey from adolescence is a perilous one, containing a number of formidable barriers to making a successful transition to the adult economic and social world" (p. 38). It is important to examine how adolescents explore, and feel committed to, certain career options. Understanding more about how career identity development relates to adolescent adjustment is a worthy goal.

Religious Identity

The relationship of religious identity to adolescent adjustment has received little attention in the literature. Current literature suggests that adolescence is an important time for changes in both religious beliefs and involvement. An estimated 95% of adolescents report that they believe in God (Farel, 1982). In a 1991 national survey of high school seniors, 85% indicated a religious preference, and over half indicated that religion was at least "pretty important" in their lives, a rate that was higher among females (62%) than males (53%). However, fewer than one-third stated that they attended organized religious services at least once a week (Johnston, Bachman, O'Malley, in press).

Additional research on religious identity development during adolescence is needed, especially given the increasing recognition of the healthy correlates of religious commitment during adolescence. Thomas and Carver (1990), in a review of research on religion and social competence, found that higher religiosity levels were associated with higher levels of adjustment and social competence. Likewise religious commitment is negatively associated with substance use (Amoateng and Bahr, 1986) and delinquency (Elifson, Peterson, and Hadaway, 1983). Given this relationship, religious identity loyalties, exploration, and continuity may play an important role in buffering urban adolescents against stress.

Ethnic Identity

Identity development may be a more complex process for minority or disadvantaged youth, in that these adolescents must struggle to integrate what it means not only to live in their society, but also what it means to belong to a specific group within this society (Beale Spencer, 1990). However, as previously suggested, the role of identity development for disadvantaged or minority youth has not been examined extensively. In a study of 237 low-income, urban, black high school adolescents, Watson and Protinsky (1991) found that most black adolescents were categorized in either moratorium or achievement statuses rather than foreclosure. Females were slightly more likely to be identity-achieved than male high school students. Although this research provides a descriptive analysis, it does not reveal how individuals in each status make decisions or cope with life circumstances.

It has been suggested by several authors that traditional measures of identity development may not accurately assess identity development among minority populations. In a critique similar to Gilligan's (1977) argument that traditional paradigms of moral development may not accurately describe the experiences of women, Phinney (1989) maintains that traditional theories of identity development may be insensitive to the unique life circumstances of minority adolescents. Phinney's ideas are based on those of Erikson (1968), who maintains that members of an "oppressed and exploited minority" (p. 303) may begin to internalize the dominant culture's opinions of that minority group, a process which leads to lowered feelings of worth, as well as development of a "negative identity."

Phinney (1990) stresses the need to examine how positive conceptions of one's own identity are developed and maintained. Based on Marcia's (1966, 1980) typology of identity statuses, Phinney developed a framework for ethnic identity development, which can be applied to many ethnic groups. Phinney suggests that adolescents move from at first accepting the values of the dominant culture, to a period of active exploration, similar to Marcia's moratorium. This moratorium can often result in a firmly held "clear, secure understanding and acceptance of one's own ethnicity" (p. 38), in which the adolescent develops a mature ethnic identity.

In a qualitative study of 91 Asian, Black, and Hispanic tenth-graders which examined ethnic identity under this framework, Phinney (1989) found that about one fourth of the adolescents had not explored their identity, one quarter were in an active period of exploration, and the remaining quarter were identity-achieved. No significant class, gender, or ethnic differences were present in the responses. The study also found that adolescents with ethnic identity-achievement scored higher on overall measures of identity and self-concept and adjustment than those without an ethnic-achieved identity, which means that ethnic identity achievement may serve as a protective factor.

Aries and Moorehead (1989), examined ethnicity in a study of 40 black junior and senior-high school students. Identity development was examined in four content areas: religion, politics, interpersonal attitudes, and ethnicity. Respondents were asked "If you could pick only one area [out of the four] upon which to base your identity, which would you pick?" It was found that 22% did not cite a most important identity area; and 45% named ethnicity as most important (only 5% named it least important), while 39% saw occupational as most central. There were no sex differences in the study. The article highlighted the need to examine family life as another area of identity. These studies demonstrate the salience of ethnic identity development, even for whites, and these measures should be incorporated into more global conceptions of identity.

In a naturalistic study of an urban high school containing four different ethnic groups (Black, White, Hispanic, and Asian), Semons (1991) found that most adolescents perceived ethnic boundaries as fluid, that is, more important in certain situations than in others. For example, Asian and Hispanic students were more aware of their ethnicity when interacting with other members of their own ethnic groups, such as at home or with same-race friends. Black and white students, on the other hand, were more likely to concentrate on issues of race when interacting with individuals of other groups, often feeling this ethnicity in terms of discrimination or fear. Some individuals sought to deny their ethnicity altogether, as one half-hispanic and half-white female student stated, "As far as I'm concerned, I'm not white, I'm not Mexican, I'm *me*!" (p. 143).

The fluidity of boundaries may be somewhat dependent on cultural context. Waddell and Cairns (1991) found that Protestants and Catholics in Northern Ireland developed quite rigid boundaries, Catholics described themselves as Irish and Protestants as British, almost as if there were two nations living in the same space.

Although ethnic identity has begun to receive the attention it deserves, little has been done to integrate ethnic identity into other identity domains. This study will compare ethnic identity development to other role domains and seek to understand how these components relate to adolescent adjustment.

IV

Outcomes For Adolescents in Urban Poverty

PSYCHOLOGICAL WELL-BEING

When examining the relationship between identity development and adolescent adjustment, it is important to look at more than behavioral outcomes. It should not be assumed that the absence of behavioral problems is indicative of positive adjustment, given that many urban adolescents who report few or no behavioral difficulties do report higher levels of anxiety and depression (Luthar and Zigler, 1991). Psychological well-being is especially important to examine during the undergraduate years, in that, in a study of adolescents living in rural poverty, junior high school students were more likely to report problems with loneliness and depression, while senior high students demonstrated higher levels of negative behavioral outcomes (Lempers, Clark-Lempers, and Simons, 1989).

Self-Esteem, Loneliness, and Depression

Even though many theorists describe adolescence as a period marked by storm and stress (Hall, 1905; Erikson, 1968), research has not substantiated these theoretical assertions. Self-esteem appears to be relatively stable during the junior and senior high years in longitudinal studies (Alsaker, 1989; Simmons and Blyth, 1987), as do feelings of loneliness and social dissatisfaction (Asher, Hymel, and Renshaw, 1984). Students were found, however, to report slightly higher levels of depression in junior high than when they were in senior high, indicating that some level of distress may be higher during early adolescence (Siegel and Brown, 1988).

37

Although adolescence itself does not appear to cause marked changes in psychological well-being, contextual influences are associated with differing levels of adjustment. In a large scale study of junior and senior high school students, minority students reported lower levels of self-esteem (Martinez and Dukes, 1991), suggesting that the effects of racism may lower self-esteem levels. Another study which examined race, gender, and class influences on self-esteem studied 5th, 8th, and 11th graders (Kohr, et. al., 1988) and found that high SES was associated with higher self-esteem. Racial differences were present only in low SES environments. In 5th grade whites scored higher than blacks, but this trend was reversed for 11th-grade students. Females scored higher than males in all three grade levels for low SES schools and higher in grades 8 and 11 in middle and high SES schools. A study conducted with adolescents in high poverty neighborhoods found that teens living in high poverty neighborhoods had lower self esteem, although black youth in these neighborhoods scored higher, due in part to higher religiosity and greater concern for correcting social inequalities (Moore and Glei, 1995).

Females have been found to report higher depression levels than males, and black adolescents are more likely to be depressed than whites (Comstock and Helsing, 1976). A study of junior high students found that low income adolescents reported higher depression scores than those in middle and upper classes (Schoenbach, et. al., 1982). Unfortunately these studies did not look for mediating or protective factors, but these studies do relate to findings offered by Lempers, Clark-Lempers, and Simons (1989), that economic hardship is associated with higher levels of loneliness and depression for rural adolescents .

Another study which looked at contextual differences in well-being found that blacks in racially segregated southern schools reported higher levels of adjustment than blacks in racially mixed schools (Powell, 1985). Powell suggests that this may be due to a higher level of cohesiveness in communities with racially segregated schools.

Future Time Perspective

Lewin (1939) describes future time perspective (FTP) as how a person views his or her psychological future as well as his or her psychological past. Blinn and Pike (1989) indicate that there is a certain ambiguity in discussion of FTP, in that some describe it as identity development (Erikson, 1963), others see it as a personality characteristic (Zibbel, 1971), or a cognitive schema (Heimberg, 1963).

Even though FTP has not been the subject of extensive study, it has shown to be positively correlated with personal and social adjustment and delay of gratification among adolescents, and with overall maturity among high school students (Verstraeten, 1980), and with persistence and satisfaction in achieving long term goals (Zalenski, 1987). In this study, grade level was found to be more predictive of FTP development than formal cognitive reasoning. Sex differences are evident in FTP, in that males tend to conceptualize the future in more distant terms than females (Blinn and Pike, 1989). Identity achievement was associated with higher levels of FTP (Berzonsky, Kuk, and Storer, 1993; Gillespie, Schulenberg, and Kim, 1991).

BEHAVIORAL OUTCOMES

Several behavioral outcomes will be considered in the current study. These are: substance use, delinquency, school outcomes, and other risk factors associated with sexuality and gang membership.

Substance Use

Alcohol and substance use can no longer be considered behaviors practiced by the deviant few. Over 51% of adolescents have experimented with some form of illicit drug, and 91% of adolescents have consumed alcohol by the age of 18 (US Department of Health, 1990). Alcohol and drug use are in fact becoming normative experiences for adolescents in our society.

As recent research has revealed that adolescent substance use is often related to family structure and the quality of perceived parental treatment (Dornbusch, 1985; Steinberg, 1987), considerable attempts have been made to identify which features of family life are most predictive of adolescent substance use. Several studies indicate that the type of family structure has an impact on parental discipline styles and adolescent adjustment. In a study of 7,514 adolescents, it was found that children from one-parent families have a higher rate of deviant activities even when the factors such as SES are controlled for (Dornbusch, 1985). Adolescents in single-parent families were also more susceptible to anti-social peer pressure, even after SES, sex, age, maternal employment, and family decision making styles were controlled for (Steinberg, 1987).

In a study of 2,012 adolescents, Flewelling and Bauman (1990) found that children from single-parent families report higher levels of drug usage, even when controlling for age, race, sex, and maternal education. Needle, Su, and Doherty (1990) found, in a cross-sectional study, that adolescents whose parents had divorced in adolescence had higher rates of drug use than those whose parents had divorced in childhood, or who came from intact families. Gender differences were present in this study, in that divorce had a significantly more negative impact on boys than girls, and remarriage of the custodial parent was associated with increased drug use in girls but not boys.

Not all studies however have shown family structure to be the most predictive variable of adolescent substance use. Selnow (1987) found that the quality of parent-child interaction, (i.e. how well adolescents perceived that they "get along" with their parents), was more predictive of subsequent adolescent substance use than the number of parents living at home. Another study found certain types of familial interaction to be more predictive of substance use than others. Tudor, Peterson, and Elifson (1980) found that parental closeness was more significantly negatively related to adolescent drug use than was parental discipline. In a study of 446 white and hispanic youth, it was found that parental influences were stronger than peer influences in predicting adolescent substance use (Coombs, Paulson, and Richardson, 1991), even though drug users report more peer influence than abstainers. Children with closer relationships to their parents (such as perceived ability to talk over problems, and respecting parental advice) were less likely to use drugs. Having a friend who used marijuana was the best predictor of all types of substance use, accounting for between 18 and 58 percent of the variance.

A study measuring perceptions of both adolescents and their parents, Rees and Wilborn (1983) found that mothers of drug-abusing adolescents reported less confidence in their parenting abilities, and were less likely to believe that changing their child's behavior was possible. Indirect parental control, such as pressure through guilt or anxiety, or open hostility was more associated with adolescent substance use. Setting consistent and explicit limits on adolescent activities was associated with decreased adolescent substance use.

Although the relationship between substance use and poverty is not strong, it does appear that living in a neighborhood experiencing economic hardship does place adolescents at risk. Smart, Adlaf, and Walsh (1994) found substance use to be higher in areas characterirized by poverty, as evidenced by the number of families in single parent homes and those with low incomes.

Delinquency

Adolescent delinquency is a pressing problem in America. Almost 1.4 billion juveniles are arrested annually. Over one billion dollars per year is required to maintain the juvenile justice system (Patterson, DeBaryshe, and Ramsey, 1989). Adolescents under 18 years of age account for 15.4% of arrests for violent crimes, and 33.5% of property crime arrests (Henggeler, 1989). Studies indicate that juvenile delinquents are more likely than non-delinquents to suffer problems in adulthood, such as unemployment, alcoholism, and involvement in welfare (Caspi, Elder, and Bem, 1987).

Cultural thought maintains that adolescent delinquency is a result of children not being supervised, and usually a product of "broken homes." The "broken home hypothesis" has guided much of social policy on adolescent delinquency (Farnworth, 1984). VanHooris, Cullen, Mathers, and Garner (1988) found, however, in a study of 152 adolescents in a small midwestern community, that living in a single-parent home was not significantly associated with delinquent behavior. Number of parents in the home also was not significantly related to adolescents' evaluation of parental treatment. Family functioning, however, was found to be positively correlated to all five types of delinquent behavior. The strongest influences were affection, supervision, and overall home quality. Males were more likely to be delinquents than females, and delinquent acts increased with age.

In an exhaustive review of the literature, Loeber and Dishion (1983) describe family management factors as having the best ability to predict future and current delinquency, followed by child problem behavior, and school performance. Low predictors were SES status and living in a single-parent home. These studies indicated that adolescents are helped by consistent discipline, strong support, and parental monitoring. A study of elementary school students found that poverty was only related to increased aggression for white students (Guerra, Huesmann, Tolan, and VanAcker, 1995).

Noting that more minority and low SES adolescents are arrested for delinquent offenses, but class differences did not exist in self-reporting delinquency, Larzelere and Patterson (1990) examined the role that family management plays in moderating these effects. Their longitudinal study of 206 fourth-grade boys examined the relationship between SES and delinquency, asking whether parental management (expressed by discipline and monitoring) moderated the effects of SES status on adolescent delinquency, or whether SES has a direct effect. Participants all had a high involvement in criminal activity, and were interviewed until grade 8. Parental management entirely mediated the effects of SES, and accounted for 46% of the variance, indicating that parental discipline is a stronger predictor of delinquent acts than economic hardship.

Academic Achievement

Adolescents living in poverty have very different experiences connected with school as compared to their middle and upper class counterparts. In a comprehensive review of studies on educational attainment and aspirations for impoverished adolescents, Sum and Fogg (1991) conclude that poor adolescents have weaker math and reading skills and score considerably lower on standardized tests than middle and upper class adolescents (18% versus 53% for non-poor adolescents on the Armed Services entrance exams). This finding has important implications, in that basic skills are associated with more time spent studying and desire to take more academically-oriented classes.

Poor adolescents are also less likely to see themselves going on to college (32% versus 63% for middle and upper class adolescents). Low SES adolescents are also half as likely to be involved in college preparatory programs, which are associated not only with less college attendance but with lower rates of completing high school as well.

A study of 14,700 adolescents (aged 14-21) found that family background variables, such as parental education and SES level, were most strongly associated with dropping out, a stronger predictor than racial group (Rumberger, 1983). Females were more likely to leave school because of pregnancy, and males for work-related reasons. Career aspirations decreased the likelihood of dropping out. The effects of pregnancy and career aspirations are magnified in low SES populations, in that the likelihood of a black, low SES woman dropping out is increased 40% if she has a child, but only by 4% if she comes from middle or upper levels of income.

In a longitudinal study of 475 youth who were sampled in the seventh and then the eleventh grade, it was found that whites were more likely to drop out than blacks, as well as individuals who had previously failed a grade. Cluster analyses revealed that highly aggressive individuals with low academic performance in grade seven were the most likely to drop out. SES and race were also factors, although not as strong. Seventh grade youth who subsequently dropped out were not less likely to have friends, but more likely to have friends who also dropped out. The regression analyses were capable of predicting 80% of the variance for boys and 47% for girls in predicting those who were likely to drop out (Cairns, Cairns, and Neckermen, 1989).

Academic achievement and dropping out of high school are influenced by racial and class issues. High school dropouts are distinguished by lower grades and feelings of competence in school. They are also less involved in school activities and not as interested in college. Pregnancy is the number one reason for dropping out for girls, especially in low SES populations. Males are more likely to drop out for work reasons. Drop out rates are also lower in schools where the teachers are conceived as committed, smaller school size, and schools with fewer discipline problems. It becomes evident dropping out of high school is not an isolated incident, but an ending point of a school career that has been marked by behavior problems and low achievement.

One qualitative study of gifted, economically disadvantaged adolescents identified several protective factors for poor adolescents in relation to academic achievement (Van-Tassel-Baska, 1989). These adolescents reported having encouraging parents who stressed the importance of education, as well as supportive teachers. Schools with accelerated programs were also seen as important. All the interviewed girls specifically mentioned their grandmother as a strong source of support, which suggests that extended family may play an important role for this social context. Peers were mentioned less often as being important to academic success. Personal factors mentioned were drive and independence. Several mentioned that their impoverished circumstances were inspiring because these circumstances pushed them to work harder to get out of it.

METHODOLOGICAL ISSUES

It is essential to employ a methodology responsive to the unique needs of the urban poor. Despite the importance of methodology, many studies use a somewhat simplistic or confounded approach to examining adolescents living in urban poverty. Several methodological limitations in poverty research will be discussed in this section: the unidimensionality of current definitions of poverty, minority issues, family structures and processes, middle class biases, and a lack of consensus in poverty definition.

Poverty Described as Unidimensional

A problem with past research is that disadvantaged adolescents are often grouped into a single category, ignoring the wide variations in the environments they experience. It is important to dig deeper than mere financial income and examine other aspects of context, such as urbanicity, financial stability, ability to meet basic needs, income of surrounding neighbors and community, living conditions, access to proper food and clothing, and hope for improved financial resources. The variety of experiences and environments of economically disadvantaged youth are seldom taken into account, which limits our ability to understand which aspects of economic hardship are most related to overall adjustment.

A study which did examine within group differences in economic hardship was conducted by Clark-Lempers, Lempers, and Netusil (1990). This study examined protective factors, those which serve to buffer stress, in economically disadvantaged populations from both rural and suburban contexts. It also used a more comprehensive assessment of poverty (an 11 item scale). As rural and suburban adolescents identified different reactions to economic distress, the importance of examining context is strongly highlighted in this study.

Experiences of poverty may consist of brief episodes or may be a more chronic and enduring state (Duncan and Rodgers, 1986), but this fluctuation is not accounted for in current studies on adolescence. The chronicity of poverty, as well as its severity, may be highly related to the perceived stressfulness of this environment. Broad generalizations about the experience of poverty for adolescents may be limited in both accuracy and usefulness. Unfortunately, studies examining negative life events (Caspi, Elder, and Bem, 1987), school outcomes (Patterson, Kupersmidt, and Vaden, 1990) and substance abuse (Coombs, Paulson, and Richardson, 1990) have divided individuals into low, middle, or upper class groups without even describing the process determining this distinction. This does not allow for an accurate evaluation of how changing economic resources and lifestyles influence these situations.

Minority Isues

A major methodological issue concerning poverty and its relationship to adolescent adjustment is a lack of sensitivity and attention given to minorities, a limitation which hinders child and family research as a whole. Most of this research has been conducted with white, middle-class populations, and has developed theories and research questions formulated from working with these elite groups.

Even though researchers have begun to question the generalizability of findings that do not consider racial variables (Scarr, 1988; McLoyd, 1990), several limitations exist that must be addressed before minority issues will be fully integrated into research efforts as a whole. A first limitation is that *minority issues are usually ignored in research design*. Many studies of adolescents do not include assessment of racial or ethnic groups. In studies examining parental satisfaction during adolescence (Pasley and Gekas, 1984), adolescent influences on family transactions (McDonald, 1982), and parent-adolescent relationships (Silverberg and Steinberg, 1987; Smetana, 1988), minority populations are not included at all. The same is true in studies which examine adolescents in stressful circumstances. In a study examining coping methods of hospitalized adolescents (Stevens, 1988), racial and economic variables were completely left out. This was also the case in studies of children coping with diabetes (Band, 1990), transitions after divorce (Hetherington, 1989), general coping strategies in early adolescence (Bird and Harris, 1990), and coping with negative life events (Rice, Sullivan, and Grund, 1991).

What is especially disturbing is that these studies do not describe themselves as limited to white, middle class populations, but represent their findings more universally. It cannot be assumed that coping strategies, or even the original stressors themselves, generalize across racial and class groups.

A second limitation is that *methods for describing racial groups are simplistic*. Bronfenbrenner (1977, 1986) maintains that much of research classifies race into two or three simple categories, describing this process as the "social address" paradigm. This simplistic categorization denies the wide array of individual and family experiences that could be present within different groups. One study on adolescent drug abuse described individuals as either white or non-white, and simply used race as a covariate of SES (Flewelling and Bauman, 1991). Acknowledgment of the differences in, for example, Hispanic populations would provide more sensitive portrayals of these populations, and allow within-group differences to emerge.

A third limitation to be presented is that *issues of race and poverty are often confounded*. Middle class whites are often compared to lower class blacks, and experiences of middle class blacks are often ignored. Research on Hispanic populations has also been found to concentrate on low SES populations (Morales, 1985). This almost implies that these populations are worthy of study only when they are experiencing some kind of difficulty. This is especially problematic because the majority of Black adolescents are not involved in drugs, premarital sex, or dropping out of school (Sum and Fogg, 1991), so the experiences of successful minority adolescents may be ignored in social science research. Efforts to improve the quality of research conducted with poor adolescents must undoubtedly grapple with the issue of race. A concerted effort to simultaneously address both issues must take place, to advance this body of research.

Morales (1984) identifies a problem in much current literature by demonstrating that most studies compare low SES Hispanics to middle class whites. Studies which examine family factors and SES usually ignore the confound of race (such as Dornbusch, 1985; Steinberg, 1987). Studies that look at family factors and SES usually ignore the confound of race. Studies that look at family structure rarely look at family dynamics, and studies that look at family dynamics rarely account for ethnic or class differences. Although many interesting findings have been generated, and the importance of family dynamics has clearly emerged as an important predictor, it is difficult to compare the relative strength of these predictive factors.

Family Structure and Processes

Although many American families no longer consist of two parents with children (Berardo, 1990), research persists in using this model for studying children and families. As lower SES families tend to be larger (Farrington and West, 1971) have extended members as part of the family unit, and be headed by single parent women (Wilson, 1986), this model is especially insensitive for this area of research. Other racial groups have been found to possess different family environments (Harrison et. al., 1990).

Most parent-adolescent research has utilized a two-parent model (Steinberg, 1987; Savin-Williams and Small, 1987; and Silverberg and Steinberg, 1987). Focus on the nuclear family denies the legitimacy of minority family patterns, and perpetuates cultural ideas that deviations from the nuclear family are detrimental to development.

Middle Class Perceived as Normative

Most studies on poor adolescents concentrate on problems, such as drugs, gangs, dropping out, etc., and ignore successful adolescents. This mimics the type of research conducted on middle class adolescents in the late 70's (Dornbusch, 1989). Studies on developmental issues are more likely to focus on middle class populations, carrying the assumption that these groups represent "normative" adolescents, and their experiences can generalize across populations.

This perception pervades much of theory and methodological construction. Theories of parent-adolescent relationships at puberty have been developed from studies of whites, such as Laursen and Collins' (1988) theory of conceptual changes during adolescence. Scales for measuring parent-adolescent interaction and communication also reflect this bias (Steinberg, 1981; Savin-Williams and Small, 1987).

For example, stress and coping measures are usually developed with white, middle class populations and then applied to their poorer counterparts. A measure designed to assess the severity of life events for ninth-grade students (Hutton, Roberts, Walter, and Zuniga, 1987) examined cohorts of honor and special education students, but did not examine racial or economically deprived groups. These items may not adequately portray the daily stressors and uplifts of poor youth.

A notable exception is a study conducted by Moseley and Lex (1990), which identified stressful life events of urban, minority youth. Although poverty was defined solely in terms of income level, stressors such as alienation from school officials, dropping out of high school, a parent being jailed, family members using drugs, and being afraid to walk in the neighborhood, among others, were identified in this 80-item checklist. This study makes an important contribution in that poor adolescents were allowed to identify their own stressors through interview and survey methods. Another strength is that adolescents both in and out of high school were recruited for participation, which is an important factor in that drop-out rates can be as high as 40% in inner-city schools (Wilson, 1986).

It cannot be assumed that theories and measures developed on white and middle class youth have universal generalizability, or even that the process of completing questionnaires and other commonly used research methods are viewed the same by different class or racial groups. Structurally different theories and methodologies are required to sensitively study this population.

Improving Research on Economic Hardship

There are several steps that could improve studies examining the relationship between economic hardship and adolescent stress and coping. A first suggestion is *to conduct more within-group studies*. Phinney (1991) calls for studies that target a very specific population, such as inner-city youth, and do not attempt to generalize beyond the specific targeted group. We need to learn more about adolescent experiences within a specific environment in order to develop accurate constructs and measures that can be used to compare the two groups. Because adolescents are more capable of manipulating their environments than children (Lewin, 1951) it becomes increasingly important to assess how individual adolescents are capable of managing a particular context in order to achieve desired goals. Noteworthy examples of this include Lempers, Clark-Lempers, and Simons' (1989) study on rural youth hit by the farmer's depression of the 1980's, and Moseley and Lex's (1990) identification of stressful life events in urban minority youth. It would be useful to apply the methodologies used in these studies to other populations.

Moving beyond problem-focused research would also be of great benefit. Many poor adolescents are not engaged in antisocial behavior (Sum and Fogg, 1991), and several manage to thrive in their environments. Learning more about adolescents who are able to achieve their goals and function in society would contribute to understanding which factors serve as protective in adolescence.

The creation of *measures and theories designed especially for disadvantaged youth* would also be a significant contribution. Works such as Wilson's (1986) Black Family Life Cycle, and Phinney's (1989) conceptualization of ethnic identity need to be encouraged and extended to other racial groups and situations. These theories and measures can be derived from qualitative, within-group studies recommended above. While it is laudable that many researchers are becoming interested in increasing understanding of disadvantaged populations, it is also obvious that we are not currently using appropriate research methodologies for these populations. Most social science research begins with a desire to understand and predict human behavior. By including the "voices" and experiences of minorities, we can add immeasurably to our understanding of not only those groups themselves, but human development in general.

SUMMARY AND IMPLICATIONS

This review reveals that it is not enough to simply reproduce research done on mainstream populations on more disadvantaged populations. Considerable attention needs also to be paid to the choice of measurement, to insure that differences in context can be revealed. It is also important to use within-group studies on disadvantaged populations, and examine normative developmental issues.

Most research concerning adolescents has concentrated on white, suburban adolescents living in two-parent families, in spite of the fact that there is reason to suspect that adolescent experiences vary according to context. This investigation focuses on several contextual factors: perceived parental treatment, and degree of economic hardship. Families from economically disadvantaged groups tend to be larger, have extended members as part of the family unit, be headed by single parent women, and exhibit different interaction and discipline styles (Wilson, 1987). These factors may all play significant roles in how developmental transitions are experienced by adolescents.

HYPOTHESES FOR CURRENT STUDY

1. Content-specific identity development will serve as a protective, or mediating factor, to both psychological and behavioral outcomes for junior high students living in the context of urban poverty.
2. The relationship between identity and behavioral outcomes will be stronger for junior high school students than the relationship between identity and psychological outcomes.
3. Relationships between content-specific identity development will be stronger for both behavioral and psychological outcomes than global assessments of identity development.

V

Method of Study

PLAN OF RESEARCH

The goal of the current research was to examine relationships among contextual factors, identity development, and psychological and behavioral outcomes. The plan of research consisted of three studies. The first was a pilot study used to create the six content-specific identity scales. There was also another miniature pilot study within the main study, which determined whether the reading level and length of the questionnaire was appropriate for urban junior high students. The third, or main, study uses these scales and examines connections between context, identity and well-being.

PILOT STUDY #1

The goals of this research were to develop six, ten-item identity scales in the areas of family, friends, school, career, religion, and ethnicity, as well as determine whether these scales possessed adequate reliability, and discriminant and convergent validity. Therefore, the first pilot study consisted of piloting six content-specific questionnaires to be used in the main study. Because much of identity research has focused on adolescents who are enrolled in college (Waterman, 1985), it was important to examine the psychometric properties of the content-specific identity scales on this population.

Sample

Forty-two students (responses from 1 individual were deleted due to missing data), all attending a large mid-western university, and enrolled in a basic survey course in computer science, participated in the study. All students enrolled in the course (n=400) were invited to participate in filling out a 25- minute questionnaire on their own time. A lottery was held to increase participation. Approximately 10% of the students completed and returned the survey. The sample was comprised of 17% males (n=7) and 83% females (n=34), consistent with the enrollment of the course. The students were 39% freshmen, 27% sophomore, 27% juniors, and 7% seniors. Mean age of the participating students was 19.8. See Table 1 for more demographic information.

Research Procedure

The survey consisted of the six, 13-item content-specific identity scales, a global identity scale (Rosenthal, Gurney and Moore, 1981) for convergent validity, and a social desirability scale (Osche and Plug, 1986) which was used to measure discriminant validity. Age, gender, race, and grade level were also measured. Participants in the college sample completed their survey at home and returned the questionnaire to their course professor. The questionnaire consisted of items regarding content-specific and global identity development, social desirability, and several demographic questions.

Measures

Content-specific identity development. Identity development scales in the areas of family, friends, academics, work, ethnicity, and religion were created.

Respondents completed six identity development scales, one for each domain. The identity development scales focused on three key constructs (fidelity, exploration, and continuity). Each scale consisted of 13 items, which tapped these three components in a given role (See Appendix B for a list of these questions).

A modified, 6-item version of the Lodahl and Kejner job involvement scale was used to create items examining the fidelity component of identity development for each of six identity domains.

Table 1

Demographic Characteristics of College Pilot Sample

	n	%
Age in years		
18	10	24%
19	11	27%
20	7	17%
21	4	10%
22	9	22%
Grade		
Freshman	16	39%
Sophomore	11	27%
Junior	11	27%
Senior	3	7%
Sex		
Male	7	17%
Female	34	83%
Race		
African American	0	0%
Hispanic	0	0%
Caucasian	41	100%
Other	0	0%
Asian	0	0%
Religious Affiliation		
Protestant	11	27%
Catholic	16	39%
Jewish	0	0%
Moslem	0	0%
No religious preference	14	34%

These questions tap levels of commitment, as well as loyalty and pride.

They do not focus on a specific set of beliefs, but on commitments and loyalties to whatever beliefs are personally held. Neither do the questions rank role fidelities, which is beneficial because adolescents may be committed to several individuals and beliefs.

Identity exploration was measured with five items original to this study. These questions examine exploration based on Grotevant's (1986) description of exploration facets: the location of the exploration, how systematic or intentional the exploration is, how much exploration is undertaken, and how focused the exploration is.

Continuity of identity was measured with five items which were also developed for this study. The measure ascertained the length of time that a particular identity commitment has been felt, as well as connections to the past and to the future. It also examined links of a particular domain to an integrated view of self.

Each of the 13 items was answered with a five-point Likert-type scale, with answers ranging from strongly agree to strongly disagree. Responses to these items were summed to determine one identity development score for each of the six content-specific domains.

Social Desirability. To test for discriminant validity of the content-specific scales, they were compared to a social desirability scale (Osche and Plug, 1986). This 16-item scale measures an individual's concern of others' opinions and the desire to always present oneself in a positive light. Sample items include, "I hide the fact that I've made a mistake" and "I feel jealous when someone succeeds when I fail." The scale had a reliability of .80 with the college students in the current study. Social desirability is commonly used as a test for discriminant validity for identity scales (Bennion and Adams, 1986), as well as other tests that measure outcomes generally viewed positive by society. It is important when using these scales to make sure that participants are not just responding to what they think the researcher would want to hear. Low or non-significant correlations indicate that answers in these scales are do not merely reflect the participant's desire to "look good."

Global identity. The identity subscale of the Erikson Psychosocial Stage Inventory (Rosenthal, Gurney, and Moore, 1981) was used for the measure of global identity. The scale is part of a larger measure examining each of Erikson's (1963) psycho-social stages of development. High scores on the identity scale express a clear sense of beliefs and personal goals, as well as confidence in achieving these goals. There are eight questions for ego-identity (sample question: "I have a clear idea of what I want to be"). There were strong correlations between the subscales of the EPSI, for example $r = .56$ ($p < .000$) between industry and identity. Construct validity was evident in the identity subscales, as the identity subscale was significantly correlated with Greenberger and Sorenson's (1974) Psychosocial Maturity Identity subscale ($r = .56$). Reliability for the current sample was .82.

This measure was selected over the Modified Erikson Psychosocial Inventory (Darling-Fisher and Leidy, 1988), even though the Modified Inventory reported slightly higher internal consistencies, for two reasons. First, it was developed specifically for school-aged children and adolescents, so the word choices were more appropriate for a junior high sample. Secondly, Rosenthal's subscales were significantly shorter than Darling-Fishers', which, due to the number of variables in this study, is an important consideration.

ANALYSES AND RESULTS

Reliability. Reliability was assessed in two ways: Cronbach's alphas and factor analyses. The goal was to obtain an internal consistency of at least .70 for each of the scales, as well as obtain to factor loadings of at least .30 for each scale item.

Exploratory factor analyses were used to select the nine items with the strongest psychometric properties from the original 13 items. In order for the scales to be comparable across domains, it was important to use parallel items in each of the six scales. Thus, the items of all six scales were examined, and items that loaded high in a *majority* of scales were selected. As can be seen in Table 2, the fourth exploration item, and the second, third, and fourth commitment items contributed consistently weak factor loadings. These items thus were deleted, and in all future analyses, the remaining nine items were used as the content-specific identity scales.

Reliabilities for the nine-item scales were all adequate, and ranged from .70 for career, to .88 for the religious scale, with an average internal consistency of .80 (see Table 3). Because of the lower reliabilities for the career and ethnic scales, several items were reworded for use in the main questionnaire.

Discriminant validity. To test for discriminant validity, the content-specific scales were compared to a social desirability scale (Osche and Plug, 1986). Social desirability, although concerned with self-definition, should not be related to the fidelity, exploration, and consistency of identity development, and several investigators have used this scale as a discriminant validity check for both the Eriksonian concepts of identity (Osche and Plug, 1986) and generativity

Table 2

Factor Loadings for Content-Specific Scales with College Pilot Sample

	Family	Student	Friendship
Fidelity 1	.59	.40	.48
Fidelity 2	.70	.61	.75
Fidelity 3	.73	.65	.59
Fidelity 4	.39	.77	.59
Exploration 1	.46	.44	.53
Exploration 2	.44	.36	.69
Exploration 3	.31	.81	.18
Exploration 4	.02	-.03	.30
Commitment 1	.79	.61	.70
Commitment 2	.18	.62	.21
Commitment 3	.75	.50	.46
Commitment 4	.26	.49	.42
Commitment 5	.50	.41	.43

	Career	Religious	Ethnic
Fidelity 1	.36	.78	.73
Fidelity 2	.68	.86	.51
Fidelity 3	.19	.88	.76
Fidelity 4	.21	.54	.42
Exploration 1	.60	.61	.21
Exploration 2	.56	.68	.20
Exploration 3	.27	.66	.66
Exploration 4	-.04	-.11	-.19
Commitment 1	.63	.69	.25
Commitment 2	.25	.27	.03
Commitment 3	.33	.71	.79
Commitment 4	.35	.20	-.07
Commitment 5	.53	.16	.08

NOTE: Underlined factor loadings represent weak item loadings.

Table 3

Characteristics of Measures for College Students (Pilot Study)

	# of Items	Mean	Standard Deviation	Possible Range	Obtained Range	Cronbach's Alpha
Identity variables						
Global identity[1]	8	27.76	4.7	8-40	14-35	.82
Role specific identity						
Family	10	36.34	6.2	10-50	23-45	.83
Student	10	31.02	6.7	10-50	12-42	.83
Friendship	10	29.98	7.0	10-50	13-42	.80
Career	10	31.78	5.5	10-50	19-41	.70
Religious	10	27.19	9.0	10-50	10-44	.88
Ethnic	10	19.93	7.2	10-50	7-37	.74
Social desirability	16	51.75	8.1	16-80	30-71	.80

[1] All available cases in the data set were used for psychometric analyses ($\underline{n} = 41$).

(McAdams). The inter-correlations of the six scales were also examined, as a low degree of intercorrelation between scales is another indicator of discriminant validity.

None of the six content-specific identity scales was significantly correlated with social desirability (as can be seen in Table 4). There were few significant relationships among the six scales, with career and student identity the only scales exhibiting a strong relationship (r=.68**). Three other scales were related at the level of a trend, friendship and student identity (r=.30), ethnic and student, (r=.30) and ethnic and friendship identity, (r=.27). These results suggest that the scales were tapping unique constructs, and that social desirability is not a determining factor in responses to these scales.

Convergent validity. The six content-specific identity scales were also compared to a global identity scale to test for convergent validity. The identity subscale of the Erikson Psychosocial Stage Inventory (Rosenthal, Gurney, and Moore, 1981) was used. Convergent validity was not evident in this sample, as none of the scales was significantly related to the measure of global identity. Another measure of global identity was added to the main study (Bennion and Adams, 1986) in order to further explore relationships between global identity and the content-specific scales. It was felt that convergent validity would more likely be present with Adam's measure, in that even though a global score is created, individual items relate to specific identity domains.

PILOT STUDY #2

It was also important to determine whether the measures were appropriate for adolescents living in urban poverty. To make this determination, four junior high school students completed a full questionnaire to test for time of questionnaire completion, readability, and comprehension.

Individuals in Boys and Girls Club in a medium-sized city were asked to fill out a questionnaire containing all the items used in the main study. Of 35 potential subjects, seven responded (20% acceptance ratio). From these respondents, two males and two females were randomly selected to participate in order to have an equal number of males and females. The individuals, three attending the 8th grade and one in 9th grade, completed the questionnaires in their own home, and were given five dollars to thank them for participating. Two research representatives were present to answer questions. The mean age of the participants was 13.5. The questionnaire examined global and content-specific identity development, perceived parental treatment, economic

Table 4

Correlation Matrix for College Students (Pilot Study)

	1	2	3	4	5	6	7	8	9	10
(1) Global Identity[1]										
(2) Family Identity	-.02									
(3) Student Identity	.03	-.01								
(4) Friend Identity	.00	-.06	.30+							
(5) Career Identity	.29+	.04	.68**	.23						
(6) Religious Identity	.04	.03	.22	-.03	.04					
(7) Ethnic Identity	-.08	.17	.30+	.27+	.18	.13				
(8) Social Desirability	.12	-.06	-.01	-.02	-.21	.25	-.04			
(9) Age	.07	.02	.00	-.15	-.18	-.17	-.19	.20		
(10) Grade	.20	.07	.00	-.15	-.11	-.17	-.19	-.08	.57***	
(11) Sex	-.21	.19	.15	.00	-.14	.04	.10	-.08	-.02	-.23

[1] Rosenthal, Gurney, and Moore (1981)

$+ = p < .10$, $* = p < .05$, $** = p < .01$, $*** = p < .001$

hardship, and behavioral and psychological outcomes. The study consisted of 174 questions. The questions that participants asked were recorded, and the students were timed to determine length of time necessary to complete questionnaire.

After administering the questionnaire, three items were reworded, based on questions asked. Time necessary to complete the questionnaires ranged from 19 to 23 minutes, which was deemed adequate for the research project.

MAIN STUDY

The main study consisted of distributing the questionnaire to adolescents in the eighth grade living in major urban areas. Two school districts in south Chicago were contacted and agreed to participate. The two middle schools both enrolled students from the sixth to eighth grades.

Sample

Eighth-grade students from two school systems participated in the research. The original intent was to involve both eighth and eleventh grade students in this study, but it was not possible to find high schools that were willing to participate. The first school was centered in a community located directly south of Chicago. This community suffered an economic decline after several steel mills closed ten years ago, resulting in a low-income urban community. All parents of the eighth-grade students enrolled in the community's middle school were mailed letters informing them of the study and asking for their permission to allow their children to participate. Of the 107 students, 57 parents responded (53%), with 84% (48) granting permission. After the questionnaires were completed, the responses of two participants were deleted due to missing data. Of the remaining 46 participants, 22 were male and 22 were female (two students had missing data for this item), with a mean age of 13.1. See Table 5 for other demographic information.

The second school was also located in south Chicago. In a procedure identical to the first school, parents of eighth-graders were mailed letters informing them of the study and asking for their permission to allow their children to participate. Of the 199 students, 79 parents responded (39%), with 56 granting permission. The participants consisted of 23 males and 32 females, with a mean age of 13.9. See Table 5 for other demographic information.

In order to ensure that both samples came from comparable environments, Chi-square analyses were run on four demographic variables. The two samples were not significantly different in terms of gender, race, or religious affiliation. However, the second sample was significantly older than the first sample ($\chi^2(3,99)$=10.77, p < .01). T-test analyses were also run on the remaining 25 variables. One other significant difference was observed, in that the first sample reported significantly higher levels of drug use ($F(45,58)$=3.75, p < .001). Because these were the only two significant differences, and no significant differences were present in the contextual variables, the two samples were judged similar enough to examine together as one group.

Research Procedure

All students took part in a paper and pencil survey measuring global and content-specific identity development, perceived parental treatment, economic hardship, and behavioral and psychological outcomes. The study consisted of 174 questions. Students whose parents either had not responded or had refused participation worked on a puzzle activity at this time. The questionnaire was anonymous, and students were informed that their participation was voluntary. The schools were visited a second time to administer the questionnaire to students absent on the first day of data collection.

Background and Context Variables

Demographic variables related to adolescent adjustment were examined. Age, gender, race, and religious affiliation were each measured with one question. Two contextual variables were examined in this study: economic hardship and perceived parental treatment.

Economic hardship was assessed with a 11-item scale based on work done by Lempers, Clark-Lempers, and Simons (1989). This scale was developed for use by adolescents, and measures changes in current and past levels of income, parental work stability, and ability to pay bills or meet basic needs. It also focuses on stability of family income. Sample items are, "During the last six months, how often did your family postpone major household purchases?" and "During the last six months, how often did your family sell some possessions?" This scale is useful in that many adolescents are not aware of the exact dollar

Table 5

Characteristics of Junior High Samples

	Sample 1		Sample 2		
	n	%	n	%	χ^2 tests between the two samples
Age in years					
12	3	7%	0	0%	$\chi^2(3,99) = 10.77$
13	34	75%	33	56%	p is < .01
14	8	18%	24	41%	
15	0	0%	2	3%	
Missing	1	1%	0	0%	
Sex					$\chi^2(1,101) = 1.1$
Male	22	48%	24	41%	p is n.s.
Female	22	48%	35	59%	
Missing	2	4%	0	0%	
Race					$\chi^2(2,100) = 5.12$
African Am.	10	22%	8	14%	p is n.s.
Hispanic	7	16%	21	36%	
Caucasian	27	60%	30	50%	
Other	1	1%	0	0%	
Asian	0	0%	0	0%	
Missing	1	1%	0	0%	
Religious Affiliation					$\chi^2(3,98) = 2.4$
Protestant	5	11%	13	22%	p is n.s.
Catholic	23	51%	27	47%	
Jewish	0	0%	0	0%	
Other	8	18%	10	17%	
No pref.	9	20%	8	13%	
Missing	1	1%	1	1%	

amount of their family's financial income, but are aware of parental behaviors concerning finances. Lempers, Clark-Lempers, and Simons (1989) argue that, for adolescents living in rural poverty, perceptions of changes of current family life, such as losing a car or the mother working outside the home for the first time, are more important than actual family resource levels. Cronbach alphas for this scale were .86 for a rural adolescent population. Economic hardship was considered as a continuous variable.

This measure was selected over objective income measures because it can be examined as a continuous variable, and because of the focus on perceptions of stability of family resources. It also examines multiple facets of economic resources, such as both necessary and luxury items.

Perceived parental treatment. Perceptions of parental treatment were assessed with a 16-item scale modified by Lempers, Clark-Lempers, and Simons (1989). This scale used items from Schaefer's (1965) Child Report of Parental Behavior Inventory, and from Roberts, Block, and Block's (1984) Child Rearing Practices Report. Validity for the original Roberts (1984) scale was tested based on comparisons of self-report measures to home observations, with a significant relationship being observed. Validity tests conducted by Schaefer (1965) found that delinquent adolescents scored significantly lower on the parental treatment scale than adolescents with non-delinquent backgrounds.

This scale taps three components of parental treatment: parental discipline, affection, and communication; all of which have been found to be strong predictors for delinquency and drug use. It also focuses on parental nurturance and disciplinary consistency. Sample items include, "My parents want to know exactly where I am and what I am doing," and "My parents try to understand how I see things." Four possible responses are offered for each item: never, sometimes, often, and very often.

Identity Development Variables

Measures of identity development examined both content-specific and global components of identity. Content-specific identity was examined in six domains: family, friends, academics, work, ethnicity, and religion.

Content-specific identity development. Respondents completed six identity development scales, one for each domain, developed during the pilot phase of this study. Each scale consisted of 9 items which were answered with a five-point Likert-type scale. Answers ranged from strongly agree to strongly disagree. Responses to these items were summed to determine one identity development score for each of the six content-specific domains.

Global identity. Two scales were used to measure global identity. The first identity subscale of the Erikson Psychosocial Stage Inventory (Rosenthal, Gurney, and Moore, 1981) was used for one measure of global identity. The 8-item scale is part of a larger measure examining each of Erikson's (1963) psycho-social stages of development. High scores on the identity scale express a clear sense of beliefs and personal goals, and confidence in achieving these goals. There are twelve questions for ego-identity (sample question: "I have a clear idea of what I want to be").

The achievement items of the ideological subscale of the Objective Measure of Ego-Identity Status (EOM-EIS; Adams, Bennion, and Huh, 1989) were used for the second measure of global identity. These items are a part of a 132-item scale which measures Marcia's (1966; 1980) four stages of identity development: diffusion, foreclosure, moratorium, and achievement. These four facets of identity development are examined in two general components: ideological and interpersonal. The achievement items were selected because they represent the degree to which an identity has been consolidated or "developed."

The ideological items were used because they were written for use with any age group (Adams, Bennion, and Huh, 1989). These eight items have six responses, ranging from strongly agree to strongly disagree.

Social Desirability. The 8-item scale used in this study was created from items in the 16-item scale used in the pilot study. This scale measures an individual's concern of others' opinions and the desire to always present oneself in a positive light. Sample items include, "I hide the fact that I've made a mistake" and "I feel jealous when someone succeeds when I fail."

Psychological Outcomes

Luthar and Zigler (1991) note that many adolescents, deemed resilient because they do not engage in outwardly destructive behaviors, still suffer from internal feelings of loneliness and depression. Thus, it was important to measure psychological outcome variables.

Self-esteem. The Rosenberg Self-esteem Scale (Rosenberg, 1979) is a 10-item Guttman scale designed to assess individuals' sense of self-esteem. Respondents are asked to strongly agree, agree, disagree, or strongly disagree with a set of statements which describe themselves. Examples of items in the scale include, "On the whole, I am satisfied with myself," and "At times I think I am no good at all."

Construct validity for this scale has been examined in two ways. Self-esteem was compared to a depression index and an index of anxiety. Results indicate that self-esteem is negatively correlated with depression for both men ($r = -56$, $p < .001$) and women ($r = -.46$, $p < .001$). In addition, self-esteem is negatively correlated with anxiety, with a correlation of $-.72$ and $-.61$ for men and women respectively ($p < .001$). This measure was selected because of its wide-spread use with a variety of adolescent populations.

Depression. Nine items from the Center of Epidemiologic Studies (CES-D) scale were used to measure levels of depression. The original measure consists of 20 questions which are responded to on a four-point Likert-type scale; responses ranging from "rarely or none of the time" to "most or all of the time." Sample items are "I thought my life had been a failure" and "I had crying spells." Several items pertained to issues not common to junior high students, such as a loss in sexual interest, and so nine items were selected that were the most relevant to junior high students.

This measure possessed excellent reliability (.85 for a population of adults, and .90 for a group of clinically depressed adults), and a four-week test-re-test reliability of .46 when used with adults. Criterion and construct validity were also adequate, in that the scale matched clinical assessments and higher scores were associated with more severe depression ratings (Husaini, et. al., 1980). This scale has been used with adolescent populations as well.

This scale was selected over Beck's (1972) measure of depression because several of the items (for example questions about lack of sexual energy) were not deemed appropriate for junior high students. Beck's (1972) scale was also longer than the CES-D. Derogatis, et. al.'s (1974) 11-item scale was also not selected because of questions pertaining to sexual interest, and because it has not been extensively used with adolescents. Even though the Children Depression Inventory (Kovacs, 1985) was developed particularly for children, it focuses on a more medical definition of depression, and the internal consistency has been as low as .70.

Loneliness was ascertained with ten items taken from Asher, Hymel, and Renshaw's (1984) 14-item scale, which examines feelings of social dissatisfaction and personal perceptions of peer status. Sample items include, "I can find a friend when I need to," and "I feel left out of things." Respondents pick from one of five choices ranging from always true to not true at all. Scores on the loneliness scale were related to sociometric status when used on a population of children in the third through sixth grades, based on peer nominations, and number of friends listed. This measure was selected for its strong psychometric properties, and its wide-spread use among adolescent populations (for example, Lempers, Clark-Lempers, and Simons, 1989).

Future Time Perspective. Future time perspective was measured with a three item, factor-based scale developed by Gillespie, Schulenberg, and Kim (1991). This scale taps adolescents' feelings of hope by asking about clarity of perceived future, optimism regarding future, and comparison of future to present . Correlations among the items ranged from .11 to .32, and all were significant at the .01 level in a sample of college students.

Behavioral Outcomes

The behavioral outcomes of interest are substance use, delinquency, and poor academic achievement. These were selected because they represent behaviors characteristic of adolescents who are under high stress, or are not demonstrating high levels of competence (Luthar and Zigler, 1991).

Substance use. The Substance Usage Index (Selnow, 1987) indicates the frequency of drug and alcohol use, as measured by self-report. It consists of five questions, which ask, "Which of the following describes how often you smoke marijuana?, alcohol?, beer?, or other drugs?" This format is beneficial in that it shows frequencies of several different types of drug use, so it reveals a range of behaviors as well as depth of those behaviors. There are six responses ranging from "never use" to "use substance every day." This measure was selected because more official reports, such as police records have been shown to possess racial bias (Morales, 1984), and self-report measures are more likely to result in honest reports if they are anonymous.

Delinquency. Elliott, Huizinga, and Ageton's (1985) Self-report Delinquency scale indicates frequencies of several types of delinquency, and nine items were taken from this scale. Self-report methods are beneficial for this population in that poor and minority adolescents tend to be over-represented in police records, and class differences disappear when self-report methods are used (Larzelere and Patterson, 1990). The original scale consists of 24 items which examine frequency of minor delinquent acts, as well as more serious types of delinquent behavior, and aims to measure the full range of delinquent activity.

Responses are scored by the adolescent listing the number of times he or she has engaged in an activity in the last six months. The modified version used in this study consists of nine items. Most items were deleted from the original 24 because they pertained to drug use, which was already being measured. Other items dealt with more serious offenses such as murder, or other felony offenses, and it was not believed that these behaviors would be present in this population.

A limitation with a self-report method is that blacks tend to underreport offenses more often than whites (Dunford and Eliot (1984), and that both races tend to under report serious crimes such as murder and rape. Despite this limitation, Henggeler (1989) argues that self-report is a superior method to relying on arrest records, because minorities and economically disadvantaged adolescents are grossly over-represented in these records. In his comprehensive assessment of the literature, he notes the low degree of association between official and self-report methods. Many delinquent activities, such as defacing property, rarely result in arrests, so that official records seriously under-represent true delinquency levels.

The absence of an arrest record cannot be assumed to reflect the absence of criminal activity. On the other hand, ... adolescents with multiple arrests were very likely to be serious offenders according to self-report methods... It is probably safe to assume that these youths [with multiple arrests] are involved in extensive criminal activity" (p. 15).

Academic achievement was measured by grade-point average, indicated by self-report. Students were also asked whether they received "mostly A's; mostly B's" etc., in the last grading period. This self-report method was used by Conger et. al. (1991), and is useful in ensuring confidentiality. Although accessing school records may provide more reliable information, the sensitivity of the other scales require that complete confidentiality be ensured.

VI

Results of Study

Analyses were designed to uncover which background and contextual factors were associated with identity development, and whether identity development served as a protective factor for both psychological and behavioral outcomes. They were also designed to discover whether identity is more related to behavioral or psychological outcomes for junior high school students living in urban poverty, and whether global or content-specific components of identity were more influential in explaining adolescent adjustment.

ANALYSIS OF PSYCHOMETRIC PROPERTIES

Many of the scales in the questionnaire have not been utilized with urban adolescents. Osche and Plug (1986) found that reliability scores for scales measuring global identity, as well as several outcome variables, were lower for blacks than whites. Thus, it was important to examine measures used with "non-traditional populations" carefully.

Carmines and Zellar (1979) discuss strategies for evaluating the reliability of measures. The most commonly used of these is *internal consistency*, which involves using Cronbach's alpha to examine correlations among items. As can be seen in Table 6, which summarizes the internal consistencies of all scales, internal consistencies ranged from .67 to .89.

Internal consistencies were also computed for each racial group, in order to examine whether one group obtained either consistently higher or lower alphas. Internal consistencies were comparable among the racial groups, and differences in scores were never more than 10%.

Table 6

Characteristics of Measures for Junior High Sample

	# of Items	Mean	Standard Deviation	Cronbach's Alpha
Context variables				
Economic hardship	11	16.67	4.2	.72
Perceived parental treatment	13	40.56	7.2	.72
Identity variables				
Global identity[1]	8	30.60	5.6	.72
Global identity[2]	8	29.19	5.6	.67
Psychological well-being				
Depression	9	17.25	6.2	.88
Loneliness	10	18.78	8.3	.89
Self-Esteem	10	31.38	5.9	.81
Behavioral outcomes				
Substance use	5	3.15	4.4	.77
Delinquency	9	3.70	5.0	.76
Grades	1	3.89	0.8	—

[1]Adams, Bennion and Huh, 1989

[2]Rosenthal, Gurney, and Moore, 1981

More importantly, a consistent pattern of lower scores was not present for any of the groups, indicating that a racial bias was not inherent in the group of scales.

Because some of the scales possessed a borderline adequate internal consistency, it was important to conduct further tests assessing the strength of the psychometric properties. Another important evaluation tool for evaluating psychometric strength is factor analysis. Factor analyses are used by social scientists to "represent a set of variables in terms of a smaller number of hypothetical variables" (Kim and Mueller, 1978, p. 9). This analysis is useful to determine whether a single factor (or construct) underlies a larger set of items, or whether multiple factors are represented in a measure (Harman, 1967). Confirmatory factor analyses were used to analyze all the measures, with one factor being hypothesized for each scale. As suggested by Kim and Mueller (1978), the χ^2/degrees of freedom ratio should be close to two for each scale.

Confirmatory factor analyses were conducted on all the established scales, paying particular attention to four scales that possessed borderline adequate internal consistencies. The four scales having internal consistencies of lower than .75 were both global identity scales, the economic hardship scale and the perceived parental treatment scale.

Both global identity scales had a χ^2/df ratio of less than two, indicating adequate goodness of fit for the model. The χ^2/df ratio for the Rosenthal scale of global identity was $40.78/20 = 2.0$, and the χ^2/df for Adam's measure of global identity was $23.42/20 = 1.2$. The perceived parental treatment also had a good χ^2/df ratio of $72.65/65 = 1.1$. The χ^2/df ratio for economic hardship, $99.22/44 = 2.3$, was slightly higher than two, so the factor analysis was re-run to test a two-factor model. However, the items did not load onto factors that were interpretable from a theoretical standpoint, so it was decided to keep economic hardship as one scale.

The factor loadings of these four borderline scales were examined. Factor loadings from Rosenthal's measure of global identity ranged from .17 to .88, with an average of .49. Only one factor loading was below .30. Factor loadings from Adam's measure of global identity ranged from .06 to .64. Two items were below .30. Factor loadings for the economic hardship scale ranged from .25 to .79, with an average of .43. Three of twelve items were below .30. Factor loadings for perceived parental treatment ranged from -.06 to .85, with an average of .40, with four items below .30.

The future time perspective scale did not possess an adequate factor structure (χ^2/df ratio of $12.20/3=4.1$. This was largely due to the very weak factor loading of the first item, and the lack of correlation among the items. Because of this weak factor structure and low internal consistency, future time perspective was not analyzed as an outcome variable for the current study.

The scales were also analyzed for their normality, linearity, and levels of kurtosis and skewness, as regression analyses are sensitive to deviations of normality. Skewness levels over 2.0 and kurtosis levels over 3.0 were considered problematic (Tabachnick and Fidell, 1989). None of the variables had overly high levels of kurtosis and skewness, and no significant outliers were detected for any of the scales.

Psychometric Properties of Newly Created Identity Scales

It was important to examine the psychometric properties of the newly created content-specific scales at a more in-depth level. An important component of the psychometric analyses was to examine the factor structures of the content-specific scales. It was hypothesized that the factor structure would consist of three inter-related factors for each of the six scales, which would correspond to the constructs of fidelity, exploration, and continuity.

Testing a three-factor model. As stated previously, it was hypothesized that the content-specific identity scales would consist of the three inter-related factors of fidelity, exploration, and consistency. However, factor analyses indicated that only two factors were actually present in the data set. In examining the goodness of fit of the model, indicated by χ^2/degrees of freedom ratios of less than 2, it appears that a two-factor model fits the data best. χ^2/df ratios for one-factor models ranged from 2.10 to 5.15, for two-factor models, from .87 to 2.08, and for three-factor models, .70 through 1.71. For each of the six roles, a two factor model fit the data significantly better than a one-factor model. For five roles, the two factor solution was not improved upon by a three-factor moel. In the sixth domain, ethnicity, three factors did fit the data signifdicantly better than two, but because of the scree plot, and on theoretical grounds, we chose to retain two factors. In each of the six content-specific scales, two eigenvalues had values gretter than 1.0, providing more evidence in favor of a two-factor soulution (Tabachnick and Fidell, 1989).

As can be seen in Table 7, the nine variables in the content-specific identity scales loaded onto each of the six scales in an identical pattern. This provides support for the idea that the items of each scale are grouped around two central themes. The factor for each of the six scales were quite strong; only two individual factor loadings (out of

54) were under the .30 recommended by Kim and Mueller (1978). The first factor, consisting of 4 items, included three items originally from the fidelity subscale and one item from the exploration subscale. An examination of the items suggested that these items centered around the construct of identity *fidelity*. The second factor was slightly less straightforward. It consisted of 5 items, one from the fidelity subscale and two each from the exploration and consistency subscales. These items appeared to center around the *influence* that a particular domain had for an individual. Because factor analyses seem to indicate the presence of two factors that consist of identical items in each scale, and these items make theoretical sense, the two factor-based scales of *fidelity* and *influence* will be used in all future analyses. See Appendix C for a complete list of items in both scales, for the sample scale of friendship.

In four out of six content areas, the fidelity and influence subscales were positively and significantly correlated. In the career and friendship areas, however, the subscales were negatively (although not significantly) correlated. Correlations between the fidelity and influence scales ranged from .39 to -.16 (average correlation across content areas was .23).

Other Psychometric Tests of Identity Scales

Several other psychometric tests were conducted: internal consistency, and convergent and discriminant validity. These were examined for each of the fidelity and influence subscales. Missing data were also studied in order to determine whether individuals should be deleted from the analyses.

Internal consistency. As shown in Table 8, alphas from the six fidelity subscales ranged from .61 to .75, with a mean internal consistency of .68. Internal consistences of the six influence subscales ranged from .58 to .85, with a mean internal consistency of .72.

Convergent validity was tested by comparing scores of content-specific scales to global identity scales (Rosenthal, Gurney, and Moore, 1981; Adams, Bennion, and Huh, 1989), with moderate correlations between the identity scales indicative of convergent validity. Convergent validity was adequate in the current sample; many of the scales were significantly correlated with the two measures of global identity. Two scales were significantly correlated to Rosenthal, Gurney, and Moore's (1981) measure (family, $r = .30$, $p < .001$; and career, $r = .21$, $p < .05$). Five of the six scales were also significantly correlated with the Adams, Bennion, and Huh (1989) scale. The only scale that did not

Table 7

Factor Loading Pattern for Six Content-Specific Identity Scales

	Family 1	2		Friendship 1	2
FID1	.43		FID1	.56	
FID3	.55		FID3	.49	
FID4	.89		FID4	.67	
EXP3	.22		EXP3	.45	
FID2		.50	FID2		.30
EXP1		.60	EXP1		.53
EXP2		.48	EXP2		.65
CON1		.79	CON1		.40
CON2		.45	CON2		.28

	Students 1	2		Religion 1	2
FID1	.50		FID1	.64	
FID3	.77		FID3	.68	
FID4	.62		FID4	.65	
EXP3	.46		EXP3	.63	
FID2		.41	FID2		.80
EXP1		.56	EXP1		.70
EXP2		.46	EXP2		.82
CON1		.61	CON1		.67
CON2		.49	CON2		.60

	Ethnic 1	2		Career 1	2
FID1	.60		FID1	.51	
FID3	.66		FID3	.54	
FID4	.63		FID4	.70	
EXP3	.68		EXP3	.55	
FID2		.42	FID2		.53
EXP1		.87	EXP1		.51
EXP2		.76	EXP2		.50
CON1		.72	CON1		.68
CON2		.64	CON2		.60

NOTE : See Appendix C for exact wording of items

exhibit a significant correlation was the friendship identity scale. It is understandable that the scales were more strongly correlated with the Adams, Bennion, and Huh scale, as this scale, although summed to create a global score, asks questions about specific content areas.

Discriminant validity was examined by correlating the content-specific scales with social desirability scales (Osche and Plug, 1986), with no significant correlations predicted. Inter-correlations among the scales were also examined for discriminant validity, with moderate correlations expected. Strong correlations would indicate lower discriminant validity, as subscales would then be measuring simply a strong desire to "look good." Discriminant validity was also present for the identity scales in that only one of the identity scales was significantly correlated to social desirability (family identity, $r=.21$, $p < .05$), and the inter-correlations among the content-specific scales were moderate, ranging from .04 to .36, with a mean correlation of .24.

Missing data was found for five of the participants in the study (see Appendix D for a summary of missing data). Because different individuals failed to complete different scales, their responses were kept in the data set. Individuals with missing data were not significantly different from those without missing data, except that, interestingly enough, individuals with missing data (with one exception) were Hispanic. The result of this missing data is that the sample size fluctuates (never by more than two individuals) in some of the analyses.

HYPOTHESIS I

Content-specific identity development will serve as a protective, or mediating factor, to both psychological and behavioral outcomes for junior high students living in the context of urban poverty.

To test whether or not identity development served as a mediating factor for urban adolescents, a path analytic strategy advocated by Pedhazur (1982) was utilized. To test for mediation, it is necessary to conduct a series of regression analyses. First, one should regress the mediator (identity development) on the independent variables (economic hardship and perceived parental treatment), second, regress the dependent variables (each psychological and behavioral outcome) on the independent variables of context; and third, to regress the dependent variables on both the independent and mediating variables.

Table 8
Characteristics of Content-Specific Identity Measures

	# of Items	Mean	Standard Deviation	Cronbach's Alpha
Domain-specific identity fidelity				
Family	4	16.16	3.4	.68
Student	4	14.54	3.7	.61
Friendship	4	15.15	3.5	.61
Career	4	15.59	3.5	.67
Religious	4	14.41	4.3	.75
Ethnic	4	13.58	4.2	.74
Domain-specific identity influence				
Family	5	16.33	4.0	.64
Student	5	14.14	4.3	.73
Friendship	5	14.81	3.7	.58
Career	5	15.08	4.4	.70
Religious	5	11.62	5.3	.85
Ethnic	5	14.14	5.3	.82

Baron and Kenny (1986) maintain that for mediation to be present, three conditions must be met: 1) the independent variable must be significantly related to the mediator in the first equation; 2) the independent variable must affect the dependent variables in the second equation; and 3) the mediator must be significantly related to the outcome variables in the third equation.

To restate these conditions with variables used in the current study, 1) context variables must be significantly related to identity variables in the first equation; 2) context variables must also affect psychological and behavioral outcome variables in the second equation; and 3) identity variables must be significantly related to outcome variables in the third equation.

Following the strategy suggested by Pedhazur, a series of three regression analyses were conducted. The first set of twelve regressions had the contextual variables of economic hardship and perceived parental treatment as the independent variables, and the 12 identity scales as the dependent variables. The second set of six regressions again used the context variables as independent, and the six psychological and behavioral outcome variables as dependent variables. Finally, another series of six regression analyses were performed, with the 12 identity and two context scales serving as independent variables, and the six outcome variables as dependent variables.

Examining Individual Series of Regressions

The first series of regression analyses tested the relationship between context and identity variables. Results show that the contextual variables of economic hardship and perceived parental treatment did explain significant levels of variance in four of the twelve identity scales.

The F statistic is used here to indicate whether or not the independent variables explain significant proportions of the variation in the dependent variable when the significant level of F (indicated as a p value) is less than or equal to .05, F is considered statistically significant. It should be noted that the actual R^2's were quite small (R^2's indicate proportion of variance explained), and not significant in eight of the twelve regression analyses. Perceived parental treatment was also not significantly related to any of the items. However, as a significant relationship was present in several cases, Baron and Kenny's first condition was met. There were significant associations with family fidelity ($F (2,100) = 3.0, p < .05$), career fidelity ($F (2,100) = 4.1, p <$

.01), ethnic fidelity (F (2,99) = 3.7, p < .05), and finally, religious fidelity (F (2,99) = 3.3, < .05). Economic hardship was the significant predictor in all four cases. None of the influence scales was significantly associated with the contextual variables.

The second set of regressions examined the relationships between context and psychological and behavioral outcomes. Results showed that significant relationships between context and outcomes were present for psychological, but not behavioral outcomes. Context was significantly related to self-esteem (F (2,99) = 5.1, p < .01); depression (F (2,100) = 5.3, p < .01); and loneliness (F (2,100) = 3.3, p < .05). In all three instances perceived parental treatment served as a significant predictor, with better perceived parental treatment being associated with more positive psychological outcomes. However, contextual variables were not significantly associated with substance use (F (2,100) = 0.6, p is n.s.); delinquency (F (2,100) = 1.0, p is n.s.); or grades (F (2,98) = 1.7, p is n.s.). Economic hardship was never directly associated with either psychological or behavioral outcomes.

The third series of regressions examined the relationships between identity development and psychological and behavioral outcomes, which is the third criterion advocated by Baron and Kelly (1986). In order for mediation to be present, a significant relationship must be present between identity and the outcome variables. Identity development (as measured in the 12 content-specific scales) was a significant predictor for four of the six outcome variables. *Self-esteem* was significantly related to identity development (F (14,85) = 2.7, p < .01), with for 31% of the variance accounted for. Family fidelity (beta = .29; where beta is an index of the trenght of the statistical relationship),ethnic fidelity (beta = .32) and parental treatment (beta = .21) were all positive predictors. *Depression* was also significantly related to identity (F (14,86) = 2.2, p < .01), with 26% of variance accounted for. Family fidelity (beta = -.29), ethnic fidelity (beta = -.23) and parental treatment (beta = -.28) were all negative predictors, while ethnic influence served as a positive predictor (beta = .28). *Loneliness* was not significantly associated with identity (F (14,86) = 1.5, p is n.s.).

In terms of behavioral outcomes, identity development was significantly related to *delinquency* (F (14,86) = 3.0, p < .01), accounting for 32% of overall variance. Student fidelity was a negative predictor (beta = -.27) and ethnic influence was a positive predictor (beta = .22). *Grades* were also significantly related to identity development (F (14,85) = 3.6, p < .001), accounting for 37% of all variance. Friendship (beta = .31) and student (beta = .25) fidelity were both positive predictors, while religious fidelity was a negative predictor (beta = -.22). Substance abuse (F (14,86) = 1.1, p is n.s.) was not significantly associated with identity development, accounting for 13% of overall variance.

Summary of Path Analyses

As can be seen from Figures 1-6, the effects of economic hardship were not experienced as direct effects in this sample, but were experienced indirectly, mediated by identity development. In four out of the six outcomes, this indirect effect was statistically significant. For psychological outcomes, the content areas of ethnic and family identity were important. Both ethnic (beta = .32) and family (beta = .29) fidelity were important positive predictors of self-esteem. Ethnic (beta = -.22) and family (beta = -.29) fidelity were also negative predictors of depression and interestingly enough, the influence of ethnic identity influence was positively related to depression (beta = .28). Loneliness was not significantly related to identity development.

In terms of behavioral outcomes, the domains of student, friend, ethnic background and religion were more strongly associated with outcomes. Predictors for levels of delinquency were student fidelity (beta = - .27) and somewhat surprisingly, ethnic influence (beta = .22) was positively associated with higher levels of delinquency. Grades were positively associated with friendship (beta = .31) and student (beta= .25) fidelity, and negatively by religious fidelity (beta = -.22).

Even though identity development was a significant mediator in four out of the six outcome variables, the paths from context to identity, and identity to outcomes were not always parallel. For example, economic hardship was negatively associated with religious fidelity, but religious fidelity was not related to any of the psychological outcomes. The only time that contextual relationships "flowed" through from context to a specific outcome was ethnic fidelity and self-esteem and depression, and religious and friendship fidelity to grades.

For the three psychological outcomes, perceived parental treatment was experienced as a direct relationship, but this was not the case for behavioral outcomes. Economic hardship was never a significant direct effect, indicating that the influences of poverty are filtered through other experiences and relationships. In four out of the six outcomes, the effects of economic hardship were mediated by identity development.

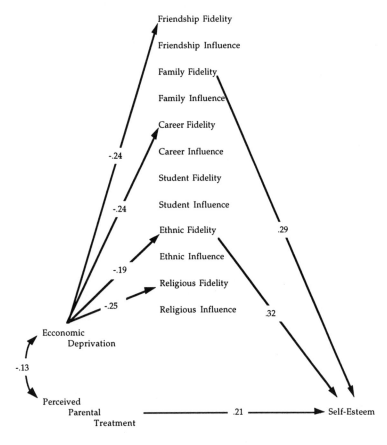

Friendship Fidelity

Friendship Influence

Family Fidelity

Family Influence

Career Fidelity

Career Influence

Student Fidelity

Student Influence

Ethnic Fidelity

Ethnic Influence

Religious Fidelity

Religious Influence

-.24

-.24

-.19

-.25

.29

.32

.21

Ecconomic Deprivation

-.13

Perceived Parental Treatment

Self-Esteem

Note: Only significant paths are shown

Figure 1
Path Analysis for Self-Esteem

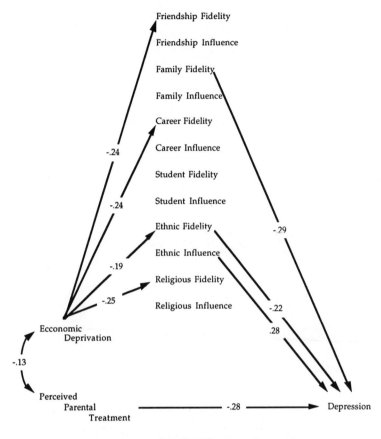

Note: Only significant paths are shown

Figure 2
Path Analysis for Depression

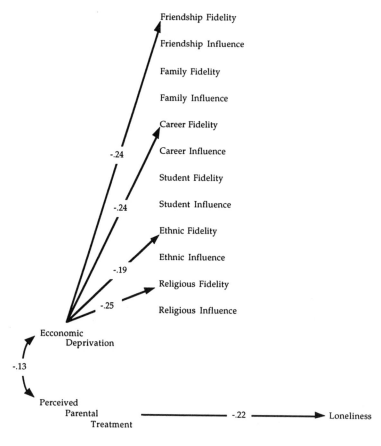

Note: Only significant paths are shown

Figure 3
Path Analysis for Loneliness

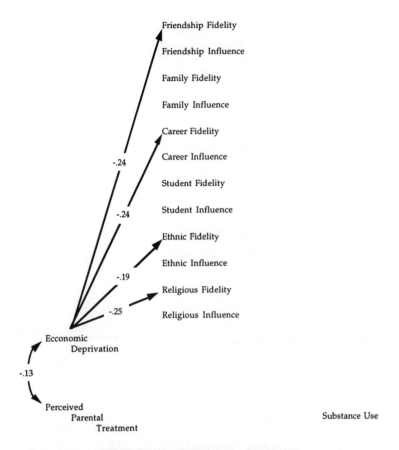

Note: Only significant paths are shown

Figure 4
Path Analysis for Substance Use

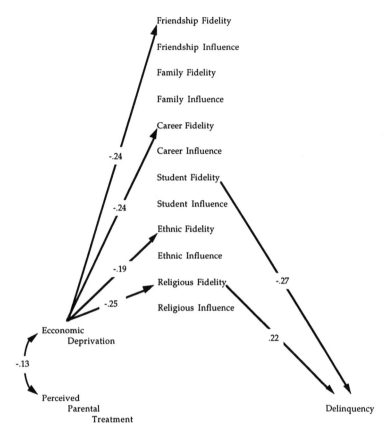

Friendship Fidelity

Friendship Influence

Family Fidelity

Family Influence

Career Fidelity

Career Influence

Student Fidelity

Student Influence

Ethnic Fidelity

Ethnic Influence

Religious Fidelity

Religious Influence

-.24

-.24

-.19

-.25

-.27

.22

Ecconomic
Deprivation

-.13

Perceived
Parental
Treatment

Delinquency

Note: Only significant paths are shown

Figure 5
Path Analysis for Delinquency

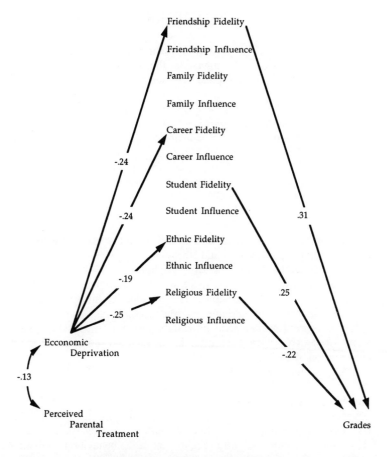

Note: Only significant paths are shown

Figure 6
Path Analysis for Grades

85

HYPOTHESIS II

The relationship between identity and behavioral outcomes will be stronger than the relationship between identity and psychological outcomes.

To test this hypothesis, a series of multiple regression analyses was performed to examine whether content-specific identity development is more related to behavioral outcomes than psychological ones. The analyses were run three times, examining differences between identity fidelity, identity influence, and the combined effect of fidelity and influence. This was done to examine whether the two measured components of identity, fidelity and influence, would exhibit unique relationships to behavioral and psychological outcomes. The full model was also included in order to see whether the scales would work together in an additive fashion. The full model is also comparable to analyses run in Hypotheses I and III.

The six content-specific identity fidelity scales were entered as independent variables in the first set, with psychological and behavioral outcomes as dependent variables. The six identity influence subscales were the independent variables in the second set, and all twelve subscales served as independent variables in the third set. Type III sums of squares were examined in order to examine the unique contribution of each variable.

Regression analyses revealed moderate support for the idea that content-specific identity was more closely related to behavioral outcomes than to psychological outcomes. The average R^2 for the three psychological outcomes was .21, while the R^2 was .27 for the three behavioral outcomes, when all twelve identity subscales were used. The R^2's were therefore slightly higher for the behavioral outcomes. However, when the fidelity and influence subscales were examined separately, the difference between behavioral and psychological outcomes became even more pronounced. R^2's were similar in terms of identity fidelity (.15 for psychological and .18 for behavioral), but for identity influence subscales, the content-specific identity scales were more strongly associated with behavioral outcomes than psychological outcomes (R^2 were .13 for behavioral, but only .04 for psychological).

Specifically, self-esteem was significantly related to the identity fidelity subscales, accounting for 23% of the variance ($F(6,95) = 4.6$, $p < .001$). Even though the identity influence scales were not significant predictors of self-esteem, when all twelve subscales were entered into the equation ($F(12,89)$ = 2.8, p < .01), an additional four percent of variance was explained.

When identity fidelity and influence subscales were entered separately, neither was a significant predictor of depression, but the twelve combined subscales ($F(12,89)$ = 1.9, p < .05) were significant, explaining 20% of overall variance. Loneliness was not significantly predicted by any combination of the identity subscales.

In terms of behavioral outcomes, two of the outcomes demonstrated significant relationships to the identity subscales: delinquency and grades. Variance in substance use was not significantly accounted for by any of the items. In terms of delinquency, all three combinations of subscales were significant. Identity fidelity ($F(6,96)$ = 4.9, p < .001) explained 23% of overall variance. Identity influence ($F(6,96)$ = 2.9, p < .01) was also significant, explaining 15% of variance. When all twelve subscales were entered into the equation, 32% of variance was explained ($F(12,89)$ = 3.6, p < .001).

When examining grades, all three combinations of items were again significant. When just fidelity items were entered, 29% of overall variance was explained ($F(6,95)$ = 6.6, p < .001). Identity influence was also significantly related to grades ($F(6,95)$ = 3.3, p < .05) accounting for 17% of the variance. When the twelve subscales were entered together, 37% of the variance was explained ($F(12,89)$ = 4.3, p < .001).

Summary. Regression analyses provided moderate support for the hypothesis that identity development was more closely related to behavioral than psychological outcomes. As can be seen in Figure 7, R^2's were higher for the behavioral outcomes than the psychological ones. When all twelve subscales are used, two behavioral and two psychological outcomes were significantly related to identity development. When the fidelity scales were used, significant relationships were present for one of the psychological outcomes and two behavioral ones. Identity influence was related to two behavioral outcomes, but none of the psychological ones.

Even though more significant relationships were present between identity development and behavioral outcomes, the differences in R^2's were not strong. This indicates that identity development may be tied to both behavioral and psychological outcomes for urban junior high school students.

HYPOTHESIS III

Relationships between content-specific identity development and both behavioral and psychological outcomes will be stronger than relationships between global assessments of identity development and outcomes.

To test this hypothesis, a similar series of regression analyses was conducted. Two sets of regressions were performed, with psychological and behavioral outcomes used as the dependent variables, and Rosenthal, Gurney, and Moore's (1981) measure of global identity as the independent variable in the first set. Adams, Bennion, and Huh's (1986) measure of identity achievement was used as the independent variable in the second set of regressions. The third regression analysis used the same dependent variables, with the twelve content-specific identity scales as independent variables. Type III sums of squares were analyzed in all three sets of regressions. The differences in R^2 for global and content-specific considerations of identity were computed to address this hypothesis.

Correlations were first conducted to examine the relationship between the independent and dependent variables. As can be seen in Table 9, Rosenthal, Gurney, and Moore's (1981) measure of global identity was significantly related to all three psychological outcomes (self-esteem, $r = .40$, $p < .001$; depression, $r = -.37$, $p < .001$; and loneliness ($r = -.35$, $p < .001$). This measure was also negatively related to delinquency ($r = -.20$, $p < .05$) and positively related to high school grades ($r = .27$, $p < .001$). Relationships between the Adam's, Bennion, and Huh (1989) measure were not significant for the three psychological outcomes, but were significantly related to grades ($r = -.21$, $p < .01$).

In the case of content-specific identity, at least one of the twelve subscales was associated with each outcome (see Table 9). Friendship, family, and ethnic fidelity were significantly and positively associated with self-esteem, as was the influence of friendship identity. Both family and ethnic fidelity were also significantly related to lower levels of depression. High levels of loneliness were also negatively related to ethnic loyalty.

In terms of behavioral outcomes, drug use was negatively correlated with the influence of both student and family identity. Delinquency was negatively associated with five of the six fidelity subscales (all except ethnic), as well as the influence of student identity. Higher

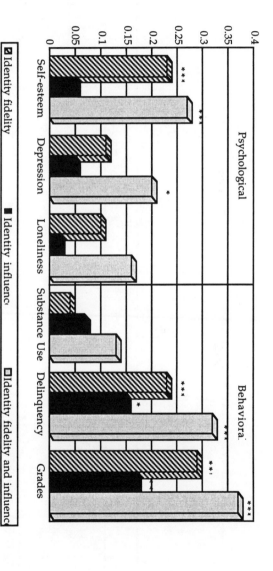

Figure 7
Comparison of the R²'s of Identity Development to Psychological and Behavioral Outcomes

Table 9

Correlations Between Identity and Outcomes

	Family fidelity	Friend fidelity	Student fidelity	Career fidelity	Religious fidelity	Ethnic fidelity	Rosenthal's identity	Adams identity
Self-esteem	.32***	.26**	.16	.16	.18	.36***	.41***	.11
Depression	-.26**	-.10	-.12	-.07	-.14	-.22*	-.37***	.07
Loneliness	-.14	-.15	.03	.07	-.11	-.19*	-.35***	.06
Substance use	.00	-.08	-.14	.01	-.07	.03	.13	-.14
Delinquency	-.30***	-.20*	-.41***	-.29**	-.28**	-.16	-.20*	-.15
Grades	.25**	.31***	.39***	.24**	.05	.33***	.27**	.21**

	Family influence	Friend influence	Student influence	Career influence	Religious influence	Ethnic influence
Self-esteem	.03	-.19*	-.07	-.13	-.06	-.05
Depression	-.02	.11	.06	.13	-.06	.13
Loneliness	.05	.00	.15	.07	.03	.02
Substance use	-.18*	-.06	-.24**	-.06	-.11	-.07
Delinquency	-.16	.01	-.24**	.12	-.02	.14
Grades	.21*	-.13	.25**	-.03	.03	.14

* = $p < .05$, ** = $p < .01$, *** = $p < .001$

grades were positively associated with five of the six fidelity scales (all except religion), as well as student and family influence.

These correlations indicate that global identity (as measured by Rosenthal, Gurney, and Moore, 1981) is closely tied to positive psychological outcomes for urban junior high school students, but also highlight the unique roles that different content areas play in specific outcomes. While a strong family identity was associated with both positive psychological and behavioral outcomes, ethnic identity was associated with positive psychological outcomes, and the development of a strong student identity was associated with positive behavioral outcomes.

In order to compare the relative strength of relationships between global and content-specific identity to selected outcomes, regression analyses were conducted and the change in R^2 was computed. As can be seen in Table 10, the R^2's were higher for the twelve subscales of content-specific identity in all cases. The average difference in R^2 was .15 with Rosenthal's measure, and .22 with Adams measure. After computing significance of change in R^2's, content-specific identity was a significantly better predictor over Rosenthal's measure in two cases: delinquency and grades. Content-specific identity was a significantly better predictor than the Adam's measure in four cases: self-esteem, depression, delinquency, and grades.

Specifically, self-esteem was related to content-specific identity ($F(12, 89) = 2.8$, $p < .01$), accounting for 27% of overall variance. Content-specific identity was also negatively related to depression ($F(12, 90) = 1.9$, $p < .05$), accounting for 20% of the overall variance.

In terms of behavioral outcomes, two regressions were significant. Delinquency was negatively associated with content-specific identity ($F(12, 90) = 3.6$, $p < .001$), accounting for 32% of the variance. Content-specific identity accounted for 37% of the variance in grade levels ($F(12, 90) = 4.3$, $p < .001$). Substance use was not significantly related to content-specific identity ($F(12, 90) = 1.1$, p is n.s.).

These results indicate the efficacy of content-specific identity assessment for urban junior high school students, particularly in behavioral content areas. They also highlight unique roles played by specific content areas.

EXPLORING RACE AND SEX DIFFERENCES

Even though gender and ethnic differences were not built into the hypotheses, it was important to explore gender and race differences in

Table 10

Regression Analyses Comparing Global and Content-Specific Measures of Identity Development

	Rosenthal's global		Adam's global		Content Specific identity	
	F	R^2	F	R^2	F	R^2
Self Esteem	$F(1,102) = 20.3$	.17***	$F(1,100) = 1.1$	.01	$F(12,89) = 2.8$	.27**
Depression	$F(1,103) = 16.1$	.14***	$F(1,101) = 0.6$	.01	$F(12,90) = 1.9$	.20*
Loneliness	$F(1,103) = 14.0$	.12***	$F(1,101) = 0.4$	.00	$F(12,90) = 1.4$	.16
Substance Use	$F(1,103) = 1.8$	.02	$F(1,101) = 1.9$	.02	$F(12,90) = 1.1$	.13
Delinquency	$F(1,103) = 4.2$	.04*	$F(1,101) = 2.2$	.02	$F(12,90) = 3.6$	.32***
Grades	$F(1,101) = 7.8$	.07**	$F(1,100) = 4.7$	.05	$F(12,89) = 4.3$	.37***
Average R^2		.09		.02		.24

the contextual, identity, and outcome variables. Three sets of 2 (sex) by 3 (race) one-way multivariate analyses of variance were conducted,with the contextual, identity, and outcome variables serving as dependent variables.

No significant racial or gender differences were present in either of the contextual variables, as the omnibus F was not significant for sex ($F(2, 97) = 0.2$, p is n.s.), or for race ($F(3, 98) = 0.7$, p is n.s.). In terms of identity variables, the omnibus F for race was significant ($F(12, 97) = 2.2$, $p < .01$). Univariate analyses revealed significant differences in friendship fidelity ($F(3, 96) = 4.5$, $p < .001$), with a mean of 16.0 for Caucasians, 15.0 for African Americans, and 13.5 for Hispanics. *A priori* tests showed that Caucasians had significantly higher friendship fidelity than did Hispanic students. The omnibus F for sex was not significant ($F(6 ,94) = 1.6$, p is n.s.).

Although no significant racial differences were present for the outcome variables (the omnibus F was not significant , $F(12,97) = 1.3$, p is n.s.), sex differences were present with the outcome variables; omnibus F was $F(6,93)=5.6$, $p < .001$. Univariate analyses revealed significant differences in depression ($F(3 ,95) = 3.6$, $p < .01$), with a mean of 18.9 for women and 15.2 for men. Significant differences were also present in delinquency ($F(3 ,95) = 3.6$, $p < .01$), with a mean of 5.6 for women and 2.4 for men. *A priori* tests revealed that females were significantly more depressed and significantly less delinquent than males.

Correlational analyses were performed which examined the relationships between the identity fidelity scales and the six outcome variables to further explore racial differences. Fidelity items were selected because previous analyses suggested that they were more closely related to the outcome variables. Several interesting racial differences were present. Family fidelity was more significantly related to outcome variables for African-American students than either Hispanic or Caucasian students. Family fidelity was positively related to self-esteem, and negatively related to substance use and delinquency. Friendship fidelity was more closely related to outcomes for Hispanic students. It was positively related to self-esteem, and negatively related to loneliness and delinquency. This is interesting in light of the fact that Hispanic students reported significantly lower levels of friendship fidelity than the other groups.

Religious fidelity was related to different outcomes for different racial groups. It was positively related to self-esteem for African-American students, negatively related to loneliness for Hispanic students, and negatively related to delinquency for Caucasians. Ethnic loyalty was associated with self-esteem for African-Americans and with grades for Hispanic and Caucasian students.

Correlational analyses were also broken down by gender, revealing several differences. Family fidelity was related to self-esteem, drugs, and delinquency for men but depression, delinquency and grades for females. Career and friendship fidelity were related to self-esteem for boys, but were not related to any significant outcome for girls. Student fidelity was associated with self-esteem and grades for girls, and delinquency and grades for boys. Ethnic identity was related to self-esteem for both sexes, and was also related to depression for boys and grades for girls. It appears from these analyses that self-esteem is more closely related to identity development for girls but the relationship is not as strong for boys. Grades are more closely linked to identity development, however, for boys than girls.

Regression analyses would have been helpful to further explore the relative strength of race and gender differences, but the small number of individuals in each group would not provide the necessary statistical power to conduct these analyses.

VII

Discussion

This study was designed to examine the developmental process of identity development for junior high students living in urban poverty. In particular, the study wished to uncover whether identity development would serve as a buffer between the context of urban poverty and psychological and behavioral outcomes. A population of 102 eighth-graders living in urban Chicago completed an anonymous questionnaire. Context was examined in two ways: economic hardship and perceived parental treatment. Identity development as expressed in six content areas was also studied: family, friendship, student, career, religion, and ethnic background. Three psychological (self-esteem, depression, and loneliness) and three behavioral (substance use, delinquency, and academic achievement) outcomes were also studied.

In summarizing the results of the study, it was found that the newly created identity scales possessed adequate psychometric properties. Internal consistency, convergent and discriminant validity tests all demonstrated that the scales performed as hypothesized. Factor structures, however, found that, instead of the scales being composed of the three constructs of fidelity, exploration, and consistency, only two factors were present in the data. The two subscales of fidelity and influence were then used in all remaining analyses.

When examining whether identity development would serve as a mediating or protective factor for junior high students living in urban poverty, it was found that in four out of six outcomes, identity development was a buffer for economic hardship. In fact, there was no direct relationship between economic hardship and any outcome; the effects of poverty were only expressed through the mediator of identity development in this study. That is to say, poverty was associated with lower levels of identity development, and lower levels of identity were associated with negative outcomes. Ethnic and family fidelity were protective factors for psychological outcomes, while student, friendship, and religious fidelity were protective for behavioral outcomes. In contrast to the first hypothesis, parental treatment, while not related to identity development, was positively associated with psychological outcomes.

Identity development was slightly more associated with behavioral outcomes than psychological ones, as predicted by the second hypothesis. Regression analyses showed that more variance was accounted for in behavioral outcomes than psychological ones. In particular, identity influence was more strongly associated with behavioral outcomes, indicating a link between the influence of identity and outward behaviors. However, the difference in variance was not strong, which indicates that identity development is tied to both psychological and behavioral outcomes for junior high school students. Another finding of the study pertains to the efficacy of examining identity across content areas, as opposed to global assessments of identity. Content-specific identity accounted for significantly higher levels of variance in four outcomes: self-esteem, depression, delinquency, and grades. Another argument for examining identity across content areas is that different identity commitments are associated with different outcomes. This highlights the utility in examining individual identity commitments when trying to explain a given outcome.

THEORETICAL AND METHODOLOGICAL IMPLICATIONS

Implications for theory and methodology will be discussed in four areas: the nature of adolescence, the nature of identity development, importance of context, and measurement issues.

Nature of Adolescence

Despite the fact that most research on identity development has focused on college students (Waterman, 1985), this study demonstrates that identity development represents an important developmental activity for much younger adolescents, even those in junior high school. The eighth-grade students in this sample who possessed higher levels of identity development were more likely to have higher self-esteem, lower levels of depression, as well as higher grades and lower levels of delinquency. These findings indicate that identity commitments are important to overall adolescent adjustment and behavior, even during early adolescence. It also shows that completing developmental tasks can be a protective factor for adolescents in stressful environments.

Early adolescents in this context also value a supportive relationship with their parents, and one in which clear discipline standards have been set. Results showed that a positive parental relationship was directly related to psychological adjustment and well-being. Perceived parental treatment did not have a direct effect on behavioral outcomes in this study.

Consistent with the findings of other studies (Peterson, Sarigiani, and Kennedy, 1991; Henggeler, 1989), the current study found that girls in this sample were more likely to be depressed, and boys were more likely to engage in delinquent activity. However, sex differences were not found in levels of identity development, indicating that males and females are equally involved in identity development during the junior high years.

Nature of Identity Development

The development of a firm set of loyalties and commitments (identity development) has shown to be an important mediating factor for adolescents living in urban poverty. In four out of the six outcomes, identity development was a significant mediator between economic hardship and psychological and behavioral outcomes. In fact, economic hardship was never directly related to any of the outcomes. This indicates that identity development is associated with context, and, even if individuals are not exhibiting direct reactions to living in poverty, it is still possible that this environment may be detrimental for their development. The findings also suggest that possessing a strong identity in this environment may be a protective factor both for how adolescents feel about themselves, as well as their outward behaviors. Identity development was also slightly more related to behavioral outcomes than psychological well-being. Whether this association changes during high school or college is yet unknown.

However, several findings suggest that identity development may come at a cost to overall adjustment. The influence of ethnic identity was associated both with higher levels of depression and delinquency (but not ethnic fidelity). It is possible that the influence of ethnic identity is accompanied by an increased awareness of racism and discrimination, which leads to more negative outcomes. Identification with an ethnic group, particularly a minority culture, may also be related to feelings of estrangement from the dominant culture, and it may take time to process and incorporate these feelings and determine identifications with both the ethnic group and society as a whole. It is also possible that what the majority culture views as a "negative outcome," such as delinquency, may be perceived as functional, or even necessary, in other contexts. Other studies on ethnic identity development (Phinney, 1990) suggest that ethnic identity is a multi-stage process, spanning adolescence and young adulthood. Longitudinal work is necessary to determine whether the effects of ethnic influence continue to result in negative outcomes through middle and late adolescence, or whether this represents only a temporary increase.

Another puzzling finding was that religious fidelity was associated with lower grades. Subsequent correlations suggest that this was only true for white individuals. These lower grades may be a result of increased involvement with religious activities, and less time spent studying, or by another intervening variable not present in this analysis. Another possible explanation for negative outcomes relating to both ethnic and religious identity is that these commitments require a certain level of introspection and self examination. While in process, this consideration may be associated with poorer adjustment. Future research efforts should continue to explore these relationships.

Even though the six content-specific identity scales were moderately correlated with each other, the six scales were each associated with separate outcomes. Family identity, particularly fidelity, was associated with self-esteem and depression. Developing a strong identity with friends was associated with higher grades. A strong identity as a student related to higher grades and lower levels of delinquency. Ethnic fidelity was strongly related to psychological outcomes of higher self-esteem and lower levels of depression, even though the influence of ethnic identity was associated with higher levels of depression. These findings show that identity commitments are not necessarily related to each other or to similar outcomes, and it therefore becomes important to examine individual commitments, when trying to understand relationships between identity and adjustment.

Importance of Context

Ecological theory advocates using "person-process-context" models of research design in order to fully understand how experiences are perceived in a given environment. Although this study provided a more in-depth look at contextual variables, and looked at the process of identity development, it is questionable whether a true person-process-context model was achieved. There was not a large enough sample size to pursue the "person" or individual variables of race or sex. Contextual research strategies, although yielding rich results, are complicated both in design and analysis, and it is hoped that future models will come closer to a true representation of the ecological model. In particular, individual contexts consist of a very complicated set of inter-related factors, undoubtedly more than were assessed in this current study. Although assessing economic hardship and parental treatment through multiple questions that focus on the *perceptions* of experiences rather than objective measures, it is also clear that other factors in this context need to be examined, such as neighborhood quality, or stressful life events.

The current study highlights the importance of mediating factors when examining a particular context. Bronfenbrenner (1986) argues that individual perceptions and experiences are often more important than the actual experiences themselves. For junior high students in the current study, the experience of poverty was not as important to adjustment, as how the experiences of poverty influenced their development (in this case identity development). The effects of a given environment, especially environments characterized by high stress, may not be expressed directly, and it therefore becomes important to examine how the effects of stressful circumstances may be exhibited in more indirect ways.

Unlike other studies that show a strong relationship between poverty and parental relationships, (Elder, Nguyen, and Caspi, 1985; Lempers, Clark-Lempers, and Simons, 1989), economic hardship and parental treatment were not significantly related in this study. This may be due to the fact that this is a within-group study. As the participants all live within the same context, the eighth graders may not view their peers to live substantially better or worse than they do. Other aspects of the environment, such as neighborhood quality, or negative life events, may be more strongly connected to parental treatment than actual economic resources, especially in an environment where students come from a similar economic background. So even though other studies show that parental treatment *mediated* the effects of poverty and outcomes, parental treatment is not even related to poverty in the current study. This again attests to the importance of examining contexts, as the relationships between parental relationship and adjustment may differ according to environment.

Measurement Issues

Earlier in this paper, several suggestions were made to improve research conducted on economic hardship. One of the suggestions was to conduct more within-group studies, in order to avoid oversimplification or distorting comparisons. This suggestion was followed for the current study, and a more in-depth measure of context was able to be assessed. This avoided using the simple "social address" model that is commonly used in poverty research, and avoided assuming that all individuals in a given context would have the same experiences. As variation was observed in both the economic hardship and perceived parental treatment scales, the advantages of digging "deeper" into context than, for example only determining the number of parents or parental salary, was found.

Another suggestion was to move beyond problem-focused research and examine normal developmental transitions. This also proved to be helpful for the current study. Identity development was significantly associated with several indicators of adolescent adjustment, which attests to the usefulness of examining these transitions.

Examining identity as expressed in specific content areas has several advantages. When global assessments of identity are compared to content-specific identity measures, the relationships between identity and psychological and behavioral outcomes were significantly stronger for four out of the six outcomes. This indicates that specific areas of identity fidelity and influence are more closely tied to adolescent well-being and adjustment than are global assessments.

Even more importantly, different identity areas were related to specific outcomes. Because family and ethnic identity were more related to psychological well-being, and friendship and student identity were more closely tied to behavioral outcomes, it appears that identity development is not unidimensional either in its formation or its relationship to adjustment and behavior. As the intercorrelations among the identity scales were only moderate, it should not be assumed that development in one area of identity will necessarily lead to development in another arena.

A final suggestion was to develop theories and measures sensitive to disadvantaged youth. Although this was attempted, it is clear that more work needs to be done in this area. The internal consistencies were only borderline adequate in some of the scales, which indicates that these measures may not work as well with this population. Although there were no significant patterns across racial groups in terms of internal consistency, the development of scales sensitive to the circumstances of minority populations will continue to be an issue.

In particular, the future time perspective scale failed as a workable scale for this population. This may indicate that the future is perceived completely differently in this context. Garbarino, Kostelny, and Dubrow (1991) suggest that urban children and adolescents often engage in a process of "terminal thinking," in which they do not even think that the future will happen. The questions about the future may have had limited meaning for these adolescents. It is important in this instance to explore how adolescents in this population feel connected to their future and what measures can facilitate thinking about the future.

It was also interesting that the only individuals with missing data (with one exception) were Hispanic. It is possible that Hispanic individuals may approach the entire process of filling out a questionnaire differently than other racial groups, had language difficulties, or this may be a more spurious finding, relating to a certain group of friends that did not have time to finish.

IMPLICATIONS OF INTERVENTION

There are several conclusions that could be useful to individuals who work with adolescents, particularly those who work with adolescents living in urban poverty. These workers should be alerted to the fact that the context of poverty can have a detrimental effect on adolescent development, namely identity development. The effects of poverty are often felt in different ways, and it should not be assumed that, even if an adolescent is not openly displaying direct effects of living in an impoverished environment, he or she is not being adversely effected by a stressful environment. Intervention programs should prioritize helping adolescents make active loyalties and commitments, as these commitments are helpful both mentally and in terms of exhibiting positive outward behaviors.

Another important implication regards the stereotypes that commonly describe adolescents in this population. Even though substance use and delinquency levels are somewhat higher than national averages, the majority of the adolescents in this study were *not* engaged in these behaviors. It is possible that adolescents living in this environment, even those not engaged in risky behaviors, may have needs for intervention. While programs to discourage substance use, delinquency, or risky sexual behavior are important for adolescents, other intervention programs are also important for adolescents not involved in these behaviors. Programs concentrating on career development or strengthening families should also be part of a comprehensive intervention.

LIMITATIONS OF STUDY

Several limitations of the study are present that could affect generalizability and should therefore be noted. As stated previously, adolescents living in poverty are not a homogeneous group. The findings of this study can not be extended beyond urban settings or the racial groups studied. While it is a contribution of the study that minority populations are studied, it is important to examine other populations as well, for the purpose of comparison. Because this study uses an original measure of identity development, the results cannot be compared to middle-class environments.

A larger sample size would have also been helpful, in order to examine gender-by-race interaction effects within the current sample. Because an active consent strategy was used, and only half of the parents returned forms allowing their children to participate, the generalizablity of the findings is somewhat limited. Even though considerable effort was taken to obtain responses from parents, such as multiple mailings and a Spanish translation, the low response rate is a limitation of this study.

As this is a cross-sectional study, it is impossible to gain a clear understanding of what causes or predicts certain developmental outcomes. Cohort differences may well be possible, in that beliefs about religion or careers are capable of changing in a fairly short period of time. Longitudinal work is needed to truly understand the *processes* of identity development, or to use identity development to predict psychological or behavioral outcomes.

Another limitation is the high number of tests that were conducted in this study. When several analyses are run, it is possible that the null hypothesis will be rejected due to chance, rather than an actual significant difference (Moore and McCabe, 1989). However, the probability of making this Type II error may not be as great in this particular set of analyses, in that certain patterns of findings emerged in the different sets of analyses (such as perceived parental treatment as a main effect for all the psychological outcome variables). This would indicate the presence of a true difference between variables. Findings that might be more questionable are those that appeared only a few times in the sets of analyses, such as religious fidelity associated with worse grades, or ethnic influence being associated with higher levels of depression and delinquency.

A final limitation of the study is the fact that subjects were not interviewed regarding the importance of identity development. It is possible that words such as commitment and exploration meant something very different to the individuals filling out the questionnaire. For example, an individual might have attended a friend's church once in his life, and consider that exploration. Another individual might have undertaken a two-year quest where she read on all major religions and talked with representatives of those religions. Exploration obviously means something different for these two individuals. The diversity of identity fidelity, exploration, and continuity might be more accurately uncovered in interview research.

IMPLICATIONS FOR FUTURE RESEARCH

One of the main contributions of this study has been to suggest future areas of research. A first possibility is to continue psychometric work in creating content-specific identity scales. As it has been shown that different identity commitments are related to specific outcomes, there is a clear need for strong measures of content-specific identity. Future measurement work should try to strengthen the internal consistency and factor structures of items, as well as return to a three-construct model of identity (i.e. develop improved questions for the exploration and consistency constructs).

Identity is an important developmental transition facing urban adolescents, but there are other normative developmental transitions that should be studied as well. Future research should continue to move beyond problem-focused studies and examine how development is perceived and negotiated in other environments, including those characterized by high levels of stress.

Examining identity within a particular context was valuable in learning about the ways that context effects development as well as both psychological and behavioral outcomes. An extension of this research would be to examine the relationships among context, identity, and outcomes with other populations as well, such as poor rural, or suburban communities.

A final suggestion for future research is to examine identity at a more in-depth level. Qualitative interviews about specific identity commitments offer several advantages. First, they would allow individuals to name the specific commitments most salient to their lives, an especially important advantage when working with less examined populations. Secondly, individuals could describe the relationships between their identity commitments and their feelings and behaviors. This would be beneficial in determining *how* identity may serve as a protective factor.

CONCLUSIONS

The purpose of this study was to examine relationships among context, identity development, and psychological and behavioral outcomes for junior high school students living in urban poverty. The study placed special emphasis on whether identity development would serve as a mediating or protective factor for individuals living in an environment characterized by high stress. Findings indicated that, in four out of six outcomes, identity development did indeed mediate the effects of economic hardship. Perceived parental treatment affected the three psychological outcomes more directly.

Identity development was slightly more associated with behavioral outcomes than psychological ones, and identity influence in particular was associated more closely with behavioral outcomes.

Several advantages were found in measuring identity development as expressed in specific content areas. First, content-specific assessments of identity were capable of explaining more variance in both psychological and behavioral outcomes than were global measurements of identity. Secondly, because different identity areas were related to different outcomes, it is helpful to examine these individual components of identity.

Appendix A

Alternate Conceptualizations of Identity

There have been several other contributions to the area of adolescent identity development, and how it ought to be conceptualized and studied. These efforts can be organized into two broader methods of conceptualization: identity style, and efforts which tap levels of identity stability, consistency, and continuity.

Berzonsky (1989) defines identity formation as "a process in which individuals need to invest personal effort and for which they are personally responsible" (p. 123). Noting previous criticisms that identity statuses may not be stable over time, he maintains that other features of identity are more important than status. He argues that instead of focusing of the outcome of identity, which has proven to be relatively unstable, it would be more useful to examine the processes, or *style*, which an individual uses; arguing that this orientation may indeed reflect a more permanent orientation to identity formation.

Berzonsky proposes three styles (1989, 1991) useful for assessing the process of identity formation. Individuals with an *information orientation* "actively seek out, process, and evaluate relevant information before making decisions. He states that foreclosed individuals are more likely to express a *normative orientation*, and will seek to conform to the standards of either their parents or society. Individuals in diffusion represent the *diffuse orientation*, which is characterized by avoidance of problems, and procrastinating on problems and letting them build up. He also has developed other scales measuring identity commitment. In a study of white undergraduates, the styles were shown to be related to identity statuses and self-esteem measures in a theoretically meaningful way.

Although the emphasis on process is encouraging, this operationalization of identity may have limited utility. If the styles merely are matched to Marcia's identity statuses, it is difficult to see how these measures differ in any significant way. The questions are very similar on the two measures, (for example, Berzonsky's "Regarding religious issues, I know basically know what I do and don't believe" is almost identical to questions used to tap religious identity achievement by Bennion and Adams, 1984). As individuals are labeled "diffuse-oriented," their style simply becomes an outcome variable instead of a process variable. So while the emphasis to look for style or orientation may be helpful, the actual operationalization of this focus is not.

Grotevant (1987) identified five factors that will influence the outcome of identity exploration. The first is *expectation and beliefs*, or the conceptions, skills, and beliefs that the individual brings into the identity search. Second, is the nature and intensity of the *exploration*, and what hypothesis testing behaviors are used. *Investment* is the third consideration, or the degree of energy, resources, time and concern put into the search, and the immediacy of the need to conduct identity exploration. Fourth is *competing forces*, a variable describing forces that act to discourage exploration, such as a lack of financial resources, or pressure from family or society not to deviate from a given path. The final variable that affects or mediates the outcome of identity exploration is *interim evaluation*, or the individual's perception of how the goal would fit into his life. The model implies that identity development is not a static ending point, and individuals move backwards and forwards on the exploration continuum. Although these facets of exploration have not been tied into Marcia's typology, they may provide a useful way to continue to examine the exploration process.

Several researchers have re-examined Erikson's (1963) idea of stability or personal consistency. Chandler and Ball (1989) argue that having a personal sense of continuity is crucial in developing a sense of self. "All of our familiar ideas regarding the assignment of personal responsibility and all of our concerns about our own future prospects appear to rest upon the certain conviction that, despite acknowledged changes, we do somehow remain persistently ourselves" (p. 150). They cite five stages of possible self development, beginning with a static composite of attributes, and ending with "an autobiographical or narrative centre of gravity" (p. 154). In a test of suicidal and non-suicidal youth, it was found that younger adolescents (mean age 14.2) were more likely to fall in the first two stages, while older adolescents (mean age 16.4) were more likely to fall in levels 3-5 Suicidal patients scored much lower than their non-hospitalized counterparts. However, the researchers' interviewing techniques were not clearly described, and their analyses were limited to frequency distributions, so this model needs more strenuous testing.

A related component entitled "self-cohesion" was the subject of another study (Blustein and Pallidino, 1991). Self-cohesion is regarded as a forgotten component of Erikson's theory, but nonetheless important. Self-cohesion was measured with two scales, both with adequate reliability and validity. The first scale, the Goal Instability Scale, examined goal directedness, ease in attaining commitments, and a sense of self-depletion. Social Superiority was the second scale, which tapped feelings of superiority over others, need for exhibitionism, and a grandiose self-appraisal. In a study of undergraduates, it was found that goal directedness and a less grandiose perception of self was related to both the identity-achieved and foreclosed statuses.

Although this study attempted to link two areas of identity, it is not clear whether these two scales adequately represent Erikson's conception of personal continuity or sense of sameness. Goal directedness and reality of perception are not synonymous with "the accrued confidence that the inner sameness and continuity of the past are matched by the sameness and continuity of one's meaning for others" suggested by Erikson (1963, p. 61).

These alternative conceptions of identity, although they have not been studied intensively, offer several insights for this study. Berzonsky's (1986) work suggests that individuals not only make unique commitments, but arrive at these commitments through different processes. The discussion of identity stability and continuity represents an important Eriksonian component of identity.

Appendix B

Questions pertaining to fidelity

Items for the sample scale of friends are:
1) To me, my friends are only a small part of who I am (negatively scored),
2) I am very loyal to my friends,
3) The major satisfaction in my life comes from my friends,
4) Most things in life are more important than my friends (negatively scored).

Another item was taken from Bosma's (1991) Identity scale:
5) I could easily give up my friends.

Questions pertaining to exploration

Items for the sample domain of academic identity are:
1) I spend a lot of time talking with other people about my studies.
2) It is important to sit down and consider all the options that school has to offer, and then make the best choices.
3) I spend more time thinking about school than most things.
4) I don't put a whole lot of thought into what classes to take or what I want my grades to be like, I kind of go with the flow (negatively scored).
5) It's important to learn how a lot of people think about school, and then choose how I want to act for myself.

Questions pertaining to continuity

Items for the sample domain of religion are:
1) My views about religion influence the way I think about a lot of things in my life,

2) I change my mind about my religious beliefs a lot (negatively scored),

3) My religion doesn't really effect any other decisions I make (negatively scored),

4) I expect my views about religion will change when I get older (negatively scored),

5) The experiences I had as a kid have helped shape the way I currently think about my religious faith.

Appendix C

Fidelity items (for the sample case of friendship fidelity)

1. (FID1) To me, my friendships with others are only a samll part of who I am.
2. (FID3) Most things in life are more important than friends (-).
3. (FID4) I could easily give up my friends (-).
4. (EXP3) I don't put a whole lot of thought into what friends I choose, I kind of hang around with whoever is around (-).

Influence items (for the sample case of friendship influence)

1. (FID2) The major satisfaction in my life comes from friendship.
2. (EXP1) I spend a lot of time talking with other people about my friends.
3. (EXP2) I spend more time thinking about my friends than most things.
4. (CON1) My views about my friends influence the way I think about a lot of things in life.
5. (CON2) My friends don't really affect an other decisions I make (-).

References

Alsaker, F.D. (1989). Global self evaluations and perceived stability of self in early adolescence. Paper presented at the Society for Research on Child Development, Kansas City, MO: March, 1989.

Amoateng, Y.Y., & Bahr, S.J. (1986). Religion, family, and adolescent drug use. *Sociological perspectives, 29,* 1, 53-76.

Arehart, D.M., & Smith, P.H. (1990). Identity in adolescence: Influences of dysfunction and psychosocial task issues. *Journal of Youth and Adolescence, 19,* 1, 63-72.

Aries, E., & Moorehead, K. (1989). The importance of ethnicity in the development of identity of black adolescents. *Psychological Reports, 65,* 75-82.

Asher, S.R., Hymel, S., & Renshaw, P.D. (1984) Loneliness in children. *Child Development, 55,* 1456-1464.

Auletta, K. (1982). *The Underclass.* New York: Random House.

Band, E.B. (1990). Children coping with diabetes: Understanding the role of cognitive development. *Journal of Pediatric Psychology, 15,* 1, 27-41.

Baron R. M., & Kelly, D.A. (1986). The moderator-mediator variable distinction in social psychological research: Conceptual, strategic, and statistical considerations. *Journal of Personality and Social Psychology, 51,* 6, 1173-1182.

Beale Spencer, M. (1990). Development of minority children: An introduction. *Child Development, 61,* 267-269.

Beale Spencer, M., Markstrom-Adams, C. (1990). Identity processes among racial and ethnic minority children in America. *Child Development, 61,* 290-310.

Beck (1972). *Depression.* Philadelphia: University of Pennsylvania Press.

Becker, A. (1990). The role of the school in the maintenance and change of ethnic group affiliation. *Human Organization, 49,* 1, 48-55.

Bennion, M., & Adams, G. (1986). *Objective measure of ego identity status: A reference manual.* Unpublished manual.

Berardo, F.M. (1990). Trends and directions in family research in the 1980's. *Journal of Marriage and the Family, 52,* 4, 809-817.

Berndt, T. (1982). The features and effects of friendship in early adolescence. *Child Development, 53,* 1447-1460.

Berndt, T. & Savin-Williams (1990). Friendships and peer relations during adolescence. In S.S. Feldman and G.R. Elliott (Eds.) *At the threshold: The developing adolescent.*

Berzonsky, M.D. (1989). Identity style: Conceptualization and measurement. *Journal of Adolescent Research, 4,3,* 268-282.

Berzonsky, M.D. (1991). A process view of identity formation and maintenance. Paper presented at biennial conference of the Society of Research in Child Development, Seattle, WA, April, 1991.

Berzonsky, M.D., Kuk, L.S., & Storer, C.J. (1993). Identity development, autonomy, and personal effectiveness. Paper presented at the Biennial meetings of the Society for Research in Child Development, New Orleans, LA: March, 1993.

Bettes, B.A., Dusenbury, L., Kerner, J., James-Ortiz, S., & Botvin, G.J. (1990). Ethnicity and psychosocial factors in alcohol and tobacco use in adolescence. *Child Development, 61,* 557-565.

Bird, G.W. & Harris, R.L. (1990). A comparison of role strain and coping strategies by gender and family structure among early adolescence. *Journal of Early Adolescence, 10*, 2, 141-158.

Blasi, A. (1988). Identity and the development of the self. In D.K. Lapsley and F.C. Power (Eds.), *Self, ego, and identity: Integrative approaches* (pp. 226-242). New York: Springer-Verlag.

Blinn, L.M. & Pike, G. (1989). Future time perspective: Adolescents' predictions of their interpersonal lives in the future. *Adolescence, 24*, 94, 289-301.

Blos, P. (1979). *The adolescent passage: Developmental issues.* New York: International Universities Press.

Blustein, D.L., & Palladino, D.E. (1991). Self and identity in late adolescence. *Journal of Adolescent Research, 6, 3, 437-453.*

Blustein, D.L., & Phillips, S.D. (1990). Relation between ego identity statuses and decision-making styles. *Journal of Counseling Psychology, 37*, 2, 160-168.

Bolger, K.E., Patterson, C.J., Thompson, W.W., & Kuperschmidt, J.B. (1995). Psychosocial adjustment among children experiencing persistent and intermittent family economic hardship. *Child Development, 66*, 4, 1107-1129.

Bosma, H.A. (1991). Identity and adolescence: Managing commitments. In G.R. Adams, T.P. Gullotta, and R. Montemayor (Eds.) *Adolescent identity formation.* Newbury Park, CT: Sage.

Bowker, L.H. & Klein, M.W. (1983). The etiology of female juvenile delinquency and gang membership: A test of psychological and social structural explanations. *Adolescence, 18*, 72, 739-751.

Bronfenbrenner, U. (1977). Lewinian space and ecological substance. *Journal of Social Issues, 33*, 4, 199-212.

Bronfenbrenner, U. (1986). Ecology of the family as a context for human development. *Developmental Psychology, 22*, 6, 723-742.

Bronfenbrenner, U. (1989). Ecological systems theory. *Annals of Child Development, 6,* 187-249.

Cairns, R.B., Cairns, B.D., & Neckerman, H.J. (1989). Early school dropout: Configurations and determinants. *Child Development, 60,* 1437-1452.

Carmines, E.G., & Zellar, R.A. (1979). Reliability and Validity assessment. Sage University Paper Series on Quantitative Applications in the Social Sciences. Beverly Hills: Sage Publications.

Caspi, A., Elder, G.H., & Bem, D.J. (1987). Moving against the world: Life course patterns of explosive children. *Developmental Psychology, 53,* 308-313.

Christopherson, B.B., Jones, R.M., Sales, A.P. (1988). Diversity in reported motivations for substance abuse as a function of ego-identity development. *Journal of Adolescent Research, 3,* 141-152.

Clark-Lempers, D.S., Lempers, J.P., & Netusil, A.J. (1990). Family financial stress, parental support, and young adolescents' academic achievement and depressive symptoms. *Journal of Early Adolescence, 10,* 1, 21-36.

Compas, B.E. (1987). Coping with stress in childhood and adolescence. *Psychological Bulletin, 101,* 3, 393-403.

Comstock, G.W., & Helsing, K.J. (1976). Symptoms of depression in two communities. *Psychological Medicine, 6,* 551-563.

Conger, R.D., Elder, G.H., Lorenz, F.O., Simons, R.L., & Whitbeck, L.B. (1991). A family process model of economic hardship influences on adjustment of early adolescent boys. Paper presented at the Society for Research in Child Development Biennial Meeting, Seattle, Washington, April, 1991.

Connell, J.P., Clifford, E., & Crichlow, W. (1991). Why do urban students leave school? Neighborhood, family, and motivational influences. Paper prepared for research conference sponsored by the

Committee for Research on the urban underclass of the Social Science Research Council.

Coombs, R.H., Paulson, M.J., & Richardson, M.A. (1991). Peer vs. parental influence in substance use among hispanic and anglo children and adolescents. *Journal of Youth and Adolescence, 20*, 1, 73-88.

Cote, J.E., & Levine, C. (1987). A formulation of Erikson's theory of ego identity formation. *Developmental Review, 7*, 273-325.

Cote, J.E., & Levine, C. (1988). A critical examination of ego identity status paradigm. *Developmental Review, 8*, 147-184.

Cross, H.J., & Allen, J.G. (1970). Ego identity status adjustment and academic achievement. *Journal of Consulting and Clinical Psychology, 32*, 2, 288.

Csikszentmihalyi, M. & Larson, R.W. (1984). *Being adolescent.* New York: Basic Books.

Darling-Fisher, C., & Kline-Leidy, D. (1988). Measuring Eriksonian development in the adult: The modified Erikson psychosocial inventory. *Psychological Reports, 62*, 747-754.

Dellas, M. & Jernigan, L.P. (1991). Ego identity as a multidimensional construct and the development of an objective instrument for its assessment. Paper presented at Society for Research on Child Development, April, 1991, Seattle, WA.

Derogatis, L.R., Lipman, R.S., Rickels, K., Uhlenhuth, E.H., & Covi, L. (1974). The Hopkins symptom checklist (HSCL): A self-report inventory. *Behavioral Science, 19*, 1-13.

Dinitto, D.M. (1995). *Social welfare: Politics and public policy.* Boston, MA: Allyn and Bacon.

Dornbusch, S.D. (1989). The sociology of adolescence. *Annual Review of Sociology, 15*, 233-259.

Douvan, E. & Adelson, J. (1966). *The adolescent experience.* New York: Wiley Press.

Dubrow, N.F., & Garbarino, J. (1989). Living in the war zone: mothers and young children in a public housing development. *Child Welfare,48*, 3-20.

Duncan, G.J., & Rodgers, W.L. (1988). Longitudinal aspects of childhood poverty. *Journal of Marriage and the Family, 50*, 1007-1021.

Dunford, F.W., & Elliot, D.S. (1984). Identifying career offenders using self-reported data. *Journal of Research on Crime and Delinquency, 21*, 57-86.

Elder, G.H. & Caspi, A. (1988). Economic stress in lives: Developmental perspectives. *Journal of Social Issues, 44*, 3, 25-45.

Elder, G.H., Liker, & Cross (1984). Parent-Child behavior in the great depression: Life course and intergenerational influences. *Life Span Development and Behavior, 6,* 109-158.

Elder, G.H., Nguyen, T.V., & Caspi, A. (1985). Linking family hardship to children's lives. *Child Development, 56*, 361-375.

Elifson, K.W., Peterson, D.M., & Hadaway, C.K. (1983). Religiosity and delinquency. *Criminology, 21*, 14, 505-527.

Elliot, D.S., Huizinga, D., & Ageton, S.S. (1985). *Explaining delinquency and drug use.* Beverly Hills, CA: Sage.

Erikson, E.H. (1963). *Childhood and Society.* New York: Norton Press.

Erikson, E.H. (1968). *Identity: Youth and Crisis.* New York: Norton.

Erikson, E.H. (1985). *The Life Cycle Completed.* New York: Norton Press.

Erikson, E.H. (1988). Youth: Fidelity and diversity. *Daedalus*, 1-24.

Farel, A. (1982). *Early adolescence and religion: A status study.* Carrboro, NC. Center for Early Adolescence.

Farnworth, M. (1984). Family structure, family attributes, and delinquency in a sample of low-income, minority males and females. *Journal of Youth and Adolescence, 13*, 4, 349-364.

Fawzy, F.L. (1987). Family composition, socio-economic status, and adolescent substance abuse. *Addictive Behaviors, 123*, 79-83.

Fishkin, J., Keniston, K., & MacKinnon, C. (1973). Moral reasoning and political ideology. *Journal of Personality and Social Psychology, 54*, 1, 51-62.

Flewelling, R.L., & Bauman, K.E. (1990). Family structure as a predictor of initial substance abuse and sexual intercourse in early adolescence. *Journal of Marriage and the Family, 52*, 171-181.

Fullinwider, N. (1991). Adolescent identity development within the context of a triangulated family system. Presented at the Biennial meeting for the Society for Research in Child Development, Seattle, WA, April.

Gad, M. Treadwell, M.G., & Johnson, J.H. (1980). Correlates of adolescent life stress as related to race, SES, and levels of perceived social support. *Journal of Clinical Child Psychology,* 13-16.

Garbarino, J., Kostelny, K., & DuBrow, N. (1991). *No place to be a child: Growing up in a war zone.* Lexington, MA: Lexington Books.

Garmezy, N. (1983). Stressors of childhood In N. Garmezy & M. Rutter (Eds.) *Stress, coping, and development.* New York: McGraw Hill.

Garmezy, N. (1984). Stress-resistant children: The search for protective factors. In J. Stevenson (Ed.), *Recent research in developmental psychopathology,* Book Supplement No. 4, *Journal of Child Psychology and Psychiatry.* Oxford: Pergamon Press.

Garmezy, N. (1992). Resiliency and vulnerability to adverse developmental outcomes associated with poverty. In T. Thompson and S.C. Hupp (Eds.) *Saving children at risk: Poverty and disabilities.* London: Sage Publishers.

Gillespie, L.K. (1990). The relationship between religious and political beliefs and ideological identity development. Unpublished master's thesis.

Gillespie, L.K., Schulenberg, J.E., & Kim, J.R. (1991). Future time perspective and identity development among college students. Paper presented at Society for Research on Child Development, April, 1991, Seattle, WA.

Gillespie, L.K. Schulenberg, J., & Kim, J.R. (1991). Identity development and future time perspective in late adolescence. Paper presented at the Biennial meetings of the Society for Research in Child Development, Seattle, WA.

Gilligan, C. (1977). In a different voice: Women's conceptions of self and of morality. *Harvard Educational Review, 47,* 4.

Greenberger, E., & Sorensen, A.B. (1974). Toward a concept of psychosocial maturity. *Journal of Youth and Adolescence, 3,* 329-358.

Grotevant, H.D. (1986). Assessment of identity development: Current Issues and Future Directions. *Journal of Adolescent Research, 1,* 175-182.

Grotevant, H.D. (1987). Toward a process model of identity formation. *Journal of Adolescent Research, 2,* 3, 203-222.

Grotevant, H.D. (1992). Assigned and chosen identity components: A process perspective on their integration. In G.R. Adams, T.P. Gullotta, and R. Montemayor (Eds.) *Adolescent identity formation.* Newbury Park, CT: Sage.

Grotevant, H.D., & Cooper, C.R. (1987). Exploration as a predictor of congruence in adolescents' career choices. *Journal of Vocational Behavior, 29,* 201-215.

Guerra, N.G., Huesmann, L.R., Tolan, P.H., & VanAcker, R. (1995). Stressful events and individual beliefs as correlates of economic disadvantage and aggression amon urban children. *Journal of Consulting and Clinical Psycholog, 63*, 4, 518-528.

Hall, G.S. (1905) *Adolescence*, New York: Appleton.

Harman, H.H. (1967). *Modern factor analysis*. Chicago: University of Chicago Press.

Hart, D. (1988). The development of personal identity in adolescence: A philosophical dilemma approach. *Merrill-Palmer Quarterly, 34*, 1, 105-114.

Hart, D., Maloney, J., & Damon, W. (1987). The meaning and development of identity. In T. Honess and K. Yardley (Eds.) *Self and Identity, perspectives across the life-span*. London: Rutledge and Kegan Paul.

Heimberg, L.K. (1963). The measurement of future time perspective. Unpublished doctoral dissertation, Vanderbilt University, Nashville, TN.

Henggeler, S.W. (1989). *Delinquency in adolescence*. London: Sage Publishers.

Hetherington, E.M. (1989). Coping with family transitions: Winners, losers, and survivors, *Child Development, 60, 1-14.*

Howard, C.W., Broquet, A.J., & Farrell, A.D. (1991). The impact of after-school context and supervision on urban middle school youth's prosocial and problem behaviors. Paper presented at the Society for Research in Child Development Biennial Meeting, Seattle, Washington, April, 1991.

Husaini, B.A., Neff, J.A., Harrington, J.B., Hughes, M.D., & Stone, R.H. (1980). Depression in rural communities validating the CES-D scale. *Journal of Community Psychology, 8*, 20-27.

Huston, A.C., McLoyd, V.C., & Coll, C.G. (1994). Children and poverty: issues in contemporary research. *Child Development, 65*, 2, 275-282.

Hutton, J.B., Roberts, T.G., Walker, J., & Zuniga, J. (1987). Ratings of severity of life events by ninth-grade students. *Psychology in the schools, 24*, 63-68.

Johnston, L.D., Bachman, J.G., & O'Malley, P.M. (in press). *Monitoring the Future: Questionnaire responses from the nation's high school seniors, 1991.* Ann Arbor, MI: Institute for Social Research.

Jones, R.M., Hartmann, B.R., Grochowski, C.O., & Glider, P. (1989). Ego identity and substance use: A comparison of adolescents in residential treatment with adolescents in school. *Personality and Individual Differences, 10*, 3, 6, 625-631.

Josselson, R. (1987). *Finding herself: Pathways to identity development in women.* San Francisco: Jossey-Bass.

Kim., J.O., & Mueller, C.W. (1978). Introduction to factor analysis: What it is and how to do it. Sage University Paper Series on Quantitative Applications in the Social Sciences. Beverly Hills: Sage Publications.

Kim, J.R., Goldstein, A. & Jurich, J. (1991). The relationship among identity development, gender, and gender roles. Paper presented at the Biennial meetings of the Society for Research in Child Development, Seattle, WA.

Kimchi, J., & Schaffner, B. (1990). Childhood protective factors and stress risk. In L.E. Arnold (Ed.), *Childhood stress.* New York: Wiley & Sons.

Kitchener, J. (1983). Intuition, critical evaluation and ethical principles: The foundation for ethical decisions in counseling psychology. *The Counseling Psychologist, 12.*

Kohlberg, L. (1976). Moral stages and moralization: The cognitive-developmental approach. In T. Likona (Ed.) *Moral development and behavior.* New York: Holt, Rinehart, and Winston.

Kotlowitz, A. (1991). *There are no children here.* New York: Doubleday.

Kotulak, R. (1990, September 28). Study finds inner-city kids live with violence. *Chicago Tribune, 1,* 16.

Kovacs, M. (1985). The children's depression inventory. *Psychopharmacology Bulletin, 21,* 995-998.

Kroger, J. (1995). The differentiation of "firm" and "developmental" foreclosure identity statuses: A longitudinal study. *Journal of Adolescent Research, 10,* 3, 317-337.

Larsen, B., & Collings, W.A. (1988). Conceptual changes during adolescence and effects upon parent child relationships, Journal of Research on Adolescents, 3, 2, 119-139.

Larzelere, R. E., & Patterson, G.R. (1990). Parental management: Mediator of effect of socioeconomic status on early delinquency. *Criminology, 28,* 301-323.

Lempers, J.D., Clark-Lempers, D.C., & Simons, R.L. (1989). Economic hardship, parenting, and distress in adolescence. *Child Development, 60,* 25-39.

Lewin, K. (1939). Field theory & experiment in social psychology: Concepts and methods. *American Journal of Sociology, 44,* 868-896.

Lewin, K. (1951). *Field theory in social science.* New York: Harper and Row.

Lodahl, T.M. & Kejner, M. (1965). The definition and measurement of job involvement. *Journal of Applied Psychology, 49,* 24-33.

Loeber, R. & Dishion, T. (1983). Early predictors of male delinquency: A review. *Psychological Bulletin, 94,* 1, 68-99.

Loevinger, J. (1976). *Ego development.* San Francisco: Jossey-Bass.

Luthar, S.S. (1991). Vulnerability and resilience: A study of high risk adolescents. *Child Development, 62,* 600-612.

Luthar, S.S., & Zigler, E. (1991). Vulnerability and competence: A review of research on resilience in childhood. *American Journal of Orthopsychiatry, 61*, 1, 6-22.

Marcia, J.E. (1966). Development and validation of ego-identity status. *Journal of Personality and Social Psychology, 38*, 239-263.

Marcia, J.E. (1980). Identity in adolescence. In J. Adelson (Ed.) *Handbook of Adolescence.* New York: Wiley.

Marcia, J.E. (1987). The identity status approach to the study of ego identity development. In T. Honess & K. Yardley (Eds.) *Self and identity, perspectives across the life-span.* London: Rutledge and Kegan Paul.

Marcia, J.E., & Friedman, J. (1970). Ego identity status in college women. *Journal of Personality, 38*, 239-263.

Markstrom-Adams, C., & Hofstra, G. (1993). The ego-virtue of fidelity: A case study for the study of religion and identity formation in adolescence. Paper presented at the Biennial meetings of the Society for Research in Child Development, New Orleans, LA: March, 1993.

Martinez, R., & Dukes, R. (1991). Ethnic and gender differences in self-esteem. *Youth and Society, 22,* 3, 318-338.

McDonald, G.W. (1982). Parental power perceptions in the family. Youth and Society, 14, 1, 3-31.

McLoyd, V.C. (1990). The impact of economic hardship on black families and children: psychological distress, parenting, and socioemotional developing. *Child Development, 61,* 311-346.

Moore, K.A., & Glei, D. (1995). Taking the plunge: An examination of positive youth development. *Journal of Adolescent Research, 10*, 1, 15-40.

Morales, A. (1984). Substance abuse and Mexican American youth: An overview. *Journal of Drug Issues, 84,* 297-311.

Moseley, J.C. & Lex, A. (1990). Identification of potentially stressful life events experienced by a population of urban minority youth. *Journal of Multicultural Counseling and Development, 18*, 118-125.

Needle, R.H., Su, S.S., & Doherty, W.J. (1990). Divorce, remarriage, and adolescent substance abuse: A prospective longitudinal study. *Journal of Marriage and the Family, 52*, 157-169.

Newman, P.R. & Newman, B.M. (1988). Differences between childhood and adulthood: The identity watershed. *Adolescence, 23*, 551-557.

O'Connor, B.P. (1995). Identity development and perceived parental behaior as a source of adolescent egocentrism. *Journal of Youth and Adolescence, 24*, 2, 205-227.

Oshe, R., & Plug, C. (1986). Cross-cultural investigation of the validity of Erikson's theory of personality development. *Journal of Personality and Social Psychology, 50*, 1240-1252.

Papini, D.R., Sebby, R.A., & Clark, S. (1989). Affective quality of family relations and adolescent identity exploration. *Adolescence, 24*, p. 456-466.

Pasley, K. & Gekas, V. (1984). Stresses and satisfactions of the parental role. *Personnel and Guidance Journal*, 400-413.

Patterson, C.J., Kupersmidt, J.B., & Vaden, N.A. (1990). Income level, gender, ethnicity, and household composition as predictors of children's school-based competence. *Child Development, 61*, 485-494.

Patterson, G.R. & Dishion, T.J. (1985). Contributions of families and peers to delinquency. *Criminology, 23*, 1, 63-79.

Pedhazur, E. (1982). *Multiple regression analyses.* New York: Holt, Rinehart, & Winston.

Patterson, G.R., DeBaryshe, B.D., & Ramsey, E. (1989). A developmental perspective on antisocial behavior. *American Psychologist, 44*, 2, 329-335.

Peterson, A.C., Sarigiani, P.A., & Kennedy, R.E. (1991). Adolescent depression: Why more girls? *Journal of Youth and Adolescence, 20,* 2, 247-271.

Phinney, J.S. (1989). Stages of ethnic identity development in minority group adolescents. *Journal of Early Adolescence, 9,* 1-2, 34-49.

Phinney, J.S. (1990). Ethnic identity in adolescents and adults: Review of research. *Psychological Bulletin, 108,* 499-514.

Phinney, J.S. (1991). Research with ethnic minority adolescents. Paper presented at the Society for Research in Child Development Biennial Meeting, Seattle, Washington, April, 1991.

Phinney, J.S., & Tarver, S. (1988). Ethnic identity search and commitment in black and white eighth-graders. *Journal of Early Adolescence, 8,* 265-277.

Podd, M.H., Marcia, J.E., & Rubin, B.M. (1970). The effects of ego-identity status and partner perception on a prisoner's dilemma game. *Journal of Social Psychology, 82,* 117-126.

Piaget, J. (1930). *The child's conception of the world.* New York: International Universities Press.

Powell, G.J. (1985). Self-concepts among afro-american students in racially isolated minority schools: Some regional differences. *Journal of the American Academy of Child Psychiatry, 24,* 142-149.

Protinsky, H., & Walker, J. (1988). Identity formation: A comparison of problem and nonproblem adolescents. *Adolescence, 23,* 89, 67-72.

Radloff, L.S. (1977). The CES-D scale: A self-report depression scale for research in the general population. *Applied Psychological Measurement, 1,* 3, 385-401.

Rees, C.D., & Wilborn, B.L. (1983). Correlates of drug use in adolescents: A comparison of families of drug abusers with families of nondrug abusers. *Journal of Youth and Adolescence, 12*, 1, 55-63.

Rest, J.R. (1975). Longitudinal study of the defining issues of moral issues: A strategy for analyzing developmental change. *Developmental Psychology, 11*, 738-748.

Rice, K.G., Sullivan, P.A., & Grund, E.M. (1991). Moderating the effects of negative life events in late adolescence. Paper presented at the Society for Research in Child Development Biennial Meeting, Seattle, Washington, April, 1991.

Roberts, G.C., Block, J.H., & Block, J. (1984). Continuity and change in parents' child-rearing practices. *Child Development, 55*, 586-597.

Rosenberg, M. (1979). *Conceiving the self.* New York, Basic Books.

Rosenthal, D.A., Gurney, R.M., & Moore, S.M. (1981). From trust to intimacy: A new inventory for examining Erikson's stages of psychosocial development. *Journal of Youth and Adolescence, 10*, 525-537.

Rowe, I., & Marcia, J.E. (1980). Ego-identity status, formal operations, and moral development. *Journal of Youth and Adolescence, 9*, 87-99.

Rumberger, R.W. (1983). Dropping out of high school: The influence of race, sex, & family background. *American Educational Research Journal, 20*, 2, 199-220.

Rutter, M. (1987). Psychosocial resilience and protective mechanisms. *American Journal of Orthopsychiatry, 57*, 316-331.

Sabatelli, R.M. & Mazor, A. (1985). Differentiation, individual, and identity formation: The integration of family system and individual developmental perspectives. *Adolescence, 20*, 619-633.

Savin-Williams, R.C., & Small, S.A. (1986). The timing of puberty and its relationship to adolescent and parent perceptions of family interactions. *Developmental Psychology, 22*, 3, 342-347.

Scarr, S. (1988). Race and gender as psychological variables. *American Psychologist, 43*, 55-59.

Schaefer, E.S. (1965). Children's reports of parental behavior: An inventory. *Child Development, 36.*

Schenkel, S., & Marcia, J.E. (1972). Attitudes toward premarital intercourse in determining ego identity status in college women. *Journal of Personality, 40*, 472-482.

Schoenbach, V.J., Kaplan, B.H., Grimson, R.C., & Wagner, E.H. (1982). American Journal of Epidemiology, 116, 5, 791-800.

Schultheiss, D. P., & Blustein, D.L. (1994). Contributions of family relation factors to the identity formation process. *Journal of Counseling and Development, 73,* 2, 159-166.

Schweder (1982). Liberalism as destiny. *Contemporary Psychology, 27*, 5, 421-424.

Selnow, G. (1987). Parent-child relationships and single and two parent families: Implications for substance abuse. *Journal of Drug Education, 17*, 4, 315-326.

Semons, M. (1991). Ethnicity in the urban high school: A naturalistic study of student experiences. *The Urban Review, 23,* 3, 137-152.

Siegel, J.M., & Brown, J.D. (1988). A prospective study of stressful circumstances, illness symptoms, and depressed mood among adolescents. *Developmental Psychology, 24*, 5, 715-721.

Silverberg, S.B. & Steinberg L. (1987). Adolescent autonomy, parent adolescent conflict, and parental well-being. *Journal of Youth and Adolescence, 16*, 3, 293-312.

Simmons, R.G., & Blyth, D.A. (1987). *Moving into adolescence: The impact of pubertal change and school context.* New York: Aldine de Gruyter.

Smart, R.G., Adlaf, E.M., & Walsh, G.W. (1994). Neighbourhood socio-economic factors in relation to student drug use and programs. *Journal of Child and Adolescent Substance Abuse, 3,* 1, 37-46.

Smetana, J.G. (1988). Adolescents' and parents' conceptions of parental authority, *Child Development, 59,* 321-335.

Sroufe, L.A., & Rutter, M.(1985). The domain of psychopathology. *Child Development, 55,* 17-29.

Steinberg, L. (1981). Transformations in family relations at puberty. *Developmental Psychology, 17,* 833-840.

Steinberg, L. (1987). Authoritative parenting, psychosocial maturity, and academic success among adolescents. *Child Development, 60,* 1424-1436.

Stevens, J.H. (1988). Social support, locus of control, and parenting in three low-income groups of mothers: Black teenagers, black adults, and white adults. *Child Development, 59,* 635-642.

Streitmatter, J.L. (1989). Identity development and academic achievement in early adolescence. *Journal of Early Adolescence, 9,* 1, 99-116.

Sum, A.M., & Fogg, W.N. (1991). The adolescent poor and the transition to early adulthood. In P. Edelman and J. Ladner (Eds.) *Adolescence and poverty: Challenges for the 1990's.* Washington, DC: Center for National Policy Press.

Tabachnick, B.G., & Fidell, L.S.(1989). *Using multivariate statistics.* New York: Harper & Row.

Taylor, R.E. (1991). Poverty and adolescent black males: The subculture of disengagement. In P. Edelman & J. Ladner (Eds.) *Adolescence and poverty: Challenges for the 1990's.* Washington, DC: Center for National Policy Press.

Thomas, D.L., & Carver, C. (1990). Religion and adolescent social competence. In T.P. Gullotta, G.R. Adams, and R. Montemayor (Eds.) *Developing social competency in adolescence.* Newbury Park: Sage Publications.

Thompson, T. (1992). For the sake of the children: Poverty and disabilities. In T. Thompson and S.C. Hupp (Eds.) *Saving children at risk: Poverty and disabilities.* London: Sage Publishers.

Tudor, C.G., Peterson, D.M., & Elifson, K.W. (1980). An examination of the relationship between peer and parental influences and adolescent drug use. *Adolescence, 15*, 60, 783-798.

US Department of Health, (1990)

VanHooris, P., Cullen, F.T., Mathers, R.A., Garner, C. (1988). The impact of family structure and quality on delinquency: A comparative assessment of structural and functional factors. *Criminology, 26*, 2, 235-261.

VanTassel-Baska, J., & Wills, G. (1987). A three year study of the effects of low income on SAT scores among the academically able. *Gifted Child Quarterly, 31*, 4, 169-173.

Vega, W.H. (1990). Hispanic families. *Journal of Marriage and the Family, 52*, 1015-1024.

Verstraetuen, D. (1980). Level of realism in adolescent future time perspective. *Human Development, 23*, 177-191.

Voydanoff, P. (1990). Economic distress and family relations: A review of the Eighties. *Journal of Marriage and Family Therapy, 52*, 4, 1099-1115.

Waddell, N., & Cairns, E. (1991). Identity preference in Northern Ireland. *Political Psychology, 12*, 2, 962-966.

Waterman, A.S. (1982). Identity developmental from adolescence from adolescence to adulthood: An extension of theory and a review of research. *Developmental Psychology, 18*, 341-358.

Waterman, A.S. (1985). Identity in the context of adolescent psychology. In A.S. Waterman (Ed.) *Identity in Adolescence: Processes and contents.*

Waterman, A.S. (1988). Identity status theory and Erikson's theory: Commonalties and differences. *Developmental Review, 8,* 185-208.

Waterman, A.S. (1992). Identity as an aspect of optimal psychological functioning. In G.R. Adams, T.P. Gullotta, & R. Montemayor (Eds.) *Adolescent identity formation.* Newbury Park, CT: Sage.

Watson, M.F., & Protinsky, H. (1991). Identity status of black adolescents: An empirical investigation. *Adolescence, 26,* 104, 963-966.

Weinmann, L.L., & Newcombe, N. (1990). Relational aspects of identity: Late adolescents' perceptions of their relationships with their parents. *Journal of Experimental Child Psychology, 50,* 357-369.

Wilinsky, H.L. (1964). Varieties of work experience. in H. Borow (Ed.) *Man in a world at work.* Boston: Houghton Mifflin.

Williams, T.M. & Kornblum, W. (1985). *Growing up poor.* Lexington, MA: Lexington Books.

Wilson, M.N. (1986). The Black extended family: An analytical consideration. *Developmental Psychology, 22,* 2, 246-258.

Wilson, W.J. (1987). *The truly disadvantaged: The inner city, the underclass, and public policy.* Chicago: The University of Chicago Press.

Wires, J.W., Barocas, R., & Hollenbeck, A.R. (1994). Determinants of adolescent identity formation: A cross-sequential study of boarding school boys. *Adolescence, 29,* 361-378.

Zalenski, Z. (1987). Behavioral effects of self-set goals for different time ranges. *International Journal of Psychology, 22,* 17-38.

Zibbel, R.A. (1971). Activity level, future time perspective, and life satisfaction in old age. *Dissertation Abstracts International, 7,* 4198B-4199B (University Microfilms No. 71-26502.

Index